J

CHILD LIFE IN GREEK ART

A

B   C

CHILD LIFE IN GREEK ART

BY

ANITA E. KLEIN

PROFESSOR OF GREEK AND LATIN
PENN COLLEGE, OSKALOOSA, IOWA

NEW YORK

COLUMBIA UNIVERSITY PRESS

M·CM·XXXII

Printed in the United States of America
The Cayuga Press, Ithaca, New York

TO
MY SMALL
NIECE AND NEPHEWS

PREFACE

In our admiration for the achievements of the ancient Greeks in art and in literature we of the modern world are perhaps too apt to think of them as a race of supermen. In reality, of course, they were just ordinary men and women like ourselves, playing their parts in life as best they could, and, for the most part, leading very common, humdrum lives. The occasional glimpses that we catch behind the scenes reveal many a familiar figure. The unscrupulous dealer, giving short weight and measure, the daring speculator, seeking to corner the grain market, the blatant demagogue, appealing to the passions of the populace, all were to be found then as now; as, fortunately, were also the upright banker, whose word was his bond, the patriotic statesman, sacrificing his own interests to those of his country, and the incorruptible public official, who left office no richer than when he entered it. For the adult, naturally, different ages have modified, or even completely changed, the conditions of life; but the problems of childhood have remained at all periods very much the same. Even so there is a never-ending fascination, which few persons can resist, in watching the small body and the awakening mind of the child as they grow and mature. The glimpses that we obtain of children in ancient Greece are unfortunately rather few, but Miss Klein has skilfully woven the scattered threads into the web of this monograph. She has not only collected and handled her material in scholarly fashion, but has also presented her results with a sympathy and understanding possible only to one who herself loves children. It is a book that should appeal to everyone who shares that love.

CLARENCE H. YOUNG

COLUMBIA UNIVERSITY

TABLE OF CONTENTS

LIST OF ILLUSTRATIONS

INTRODUCTION

In the following sketch the purpose has been to trace life through the period of childhood only. As a result the illustrations of youths as athletes, relatively frequent in vase paintings, have been largely omitted, as well as other smaller groups, such as banquet scenes and occupations of older girls or young women. Here and there it has seemed possible to draw added information from the figures of Eros, especially numerous among the terracottas, for they frequently parallel illustrations of real children, and we assume that the artist naturally represented Eros much as he knew the Greek child. This is true also of figures which have been identified as the Dioscuri, for example, or Heracles, Perseus, and the several children of Asclepius.

So far as I know, no one has yet attempted to give a full discussion of the field; I have endeavored, therefore, as far as possible, to make a study of all the material which is at present accessible. Certain writers have undertaken to localize particular customs or practices on the basis of monuments found only in those regions. Their absence from other places may be due to accidental causes, and therefore it has seemed to me wiser to avoid definite statements in such matters.

All available material in the principal museums of America and Europe has been considered at first hand, with two exceptions—the Museo Archeologico in Florence was closed at the time of the writer's visit, and the Hermitage in Leningrad was omitted because of unsettled conditions existing there. Additional information has been gathered from the catalogues of other museums, and from publications which contain plates or detailed descriptions of objects. Where illustrations of any one thing are few, references are as complete as possible; where they are very numerous, only the best and most typical are cited. Except in unusual cases, three or four examples have seemed sufficient. A few figures may be given here by way of illustration: a small child, "swaddled" and held in the arms of an adult, occurs forty times; cradles, many of them alike, number forty also; dolls, or figures which may perhaps have served as dolls, reach a total considerably over one hundred; children with dogs beside them are almost as numerous.

Many of the objects were undoubtedly made to serve as votive offerings, rather than for actual use. They have been included here because those who were responsible for their making obviously drew upon objects and scenes from the daily life of the times. Even though the object dedicated was not the one which had actually been used by the dedicator, it at least suggested its essential features. Since, further, large numbers of these objects were found in children's graves, one is safe in assuming that they had been intimately connected with the life of these youngsters.

An important factor in a study of this sort is the obvious carelessness of execution in the case of nearly all the small vases. While the general effect is extremely lifelike, details are found to be blurred and uncertain, or are omitted altogether. In the interpretation of the terracottas one often fares no better. Many of them are of rude workmanship, and so lack detailed treatment; others, which were obviously moulded with great care originally, have suffered much from wear, and the surface modelling has, to a great extent, been lost. Certain allowances must be made, also, in the acceptance of forms due to artistic convention, as, for example, the θολία or wide-brimmed hat with conical crown, worn by girls and women. Although it is regularly moulded so as merely to rest upon the head, it seems quite certain that, as actually worn, it must have been made to fit down over the crown at least.

The attempt to designate objects in the museums by their numbers has not been uniformly successful. Some difficulties have arisen because of the varying systems of classification employed in different places, and in some museums it has been altogether impossible to obtain numbers with which to refer to the objects.

For photographs and for much helpful assistance my grateful acknowledgment is made to the following: Miss Grace Nelson, Miss G. M. A. Richter, Aziz Bey, Mr. J. D. Beazley, Mr. L. D. Caskey, Mr. Albert Gallatin, Mr. P. Kastriotes, Dr. Ernst Langlotz, Prof. Fernand Mayence, D. José Ramón Mélida, Prof. Alfred Merlin, Dr. Valentin Mueller, Prof. Ferdinand Noack, Prof. Paolo Orsi, Prof. Ernst Pfuhl, Prof. David M. Robinson, Prof. Bruno Schroeder, Prof. T. Leslie Shear, Prof. Johannes Sieveking, Mr. H. B. Walters and Dr. Robert Zahn.

I desire also to acknowledge the courtesy of the directors of museums and of the individuals who have allowed me to reproduce objects in their collections. The following publishers have kindly given me permission to make use of plates from the volumes named: F. Bruckmann, E. Pfuhl, *Masterpieces of Greek Drawing and Painting*, and Furtwängler und Reichhold, *Griechische Vasenmalerei;* Walter de Gruyter and Co., *Archäologische Zeitung* (1872), Conze, *Die Attischen Grabreliefs*, and Gerhard, *Apulische Vasenbilder*.

Finally it is my pleasant duty to express particular gratitude to Professor C. H. Young, at whose suggestion this study was undertaken. His unfailing encouragement and many helpful criticisms have been of invaluable assistance throughout the work.

INFANCY

Greek child life in its earliest stages cannot be observed without at the same time seeing the child in its relations to the mother primarily, but frequently also to the nurse. The youngest Greek child recorded is the tiny bundle seen on a painted stele—a new-born baby, apparently, held by a servant standing behind the mother's bed.[1] Here, and often elsewhere too, the child's head is protected by a pointed cap, brought well down over the ears and the back of the neck. It was apparently not fastened in any way, so it must have been rather close-fitting; occasionally the point is surmounted by a small round tuft,[2] but more frequently not.

I A

As to the exact method of clothing the small body, there is greater variety, or possibly less certainty, in the evidence at our disposal. In the majority of cases the outlines of the figure certainly suggest a child closely wrapped, although it must be admitted that often there are few or no lines to represent the winding of the swaddling band.[3] Yet there are a considerable number of terracottas which show us very clearly bands of varying widths wrapped tightly round and round. Some of them move us to hope that the babies were less uncomfortable than they seem to us. The feet may be left uncovered,[4] or the neck is free,[5] but several figures are, apparently, wrapped from tip to toe, so that nothing but the face is exposed.[6] Sometimes, it should be added, the head is left entirely bare.[7]

II A

I C

II B

While it seems safe to assume that swaddling was common, it was evidently not the only form of clothing used. Certain figures suggest a large garment or mantle, wrapped more or less loosely about the child, and a few show it hanging free below the child's feet.   In one instance it seems to extend only from the armpits down,[8] while another looks very like the infant's long dress of modern times.[9]

As for colors, the evidence which we possess is so slight that generalizations of any sort are out of the question.   However, it is interesting merely to observe that on the painted stelai, in contrast to the reddish-brown garment covering the child's body, the pointed cap is white.[10]

As the child grows older it most frequently appears entirely

III A nude,[11] or with only a cap,[12] or a small cloak in addition,[13] clasped on the right shoulder.   When the child is held by some one, a partial covering is sometimes provided by the himation of the older person.[14] One often sees the mother either standing or seated, nursing her child at the breast,[15] or simply holding it on her left arm while the baby turns its face toward hers, or nestles its head close to her neck.[16] Again, the old family nurse may often be seen, with face so wrinkled and ugly, and body so stooped that she is clearly distinguished from the mother herself.   Whether standing or seated, her head is generally

I D bent forward so that she seems to be watching her small charge intently and affectionately.[17]   Occasionally the hand of the child is so placed as to suggest that it is caressing the old nurse.[18]   That a very real affection did develop between many such individuals is only natural.   Therefore it is interesting to find a bit of evidence here and there, such as a grave stele to "Nurse Choirine,"[19] and another describing Paideusis as an "excellent nurse."[20]   One cannot doubt that these were erected by persons who felt grateful for the care they had enjoyed in their childhood.   Even greater praise is bestowed upon a certain Phanostrate, "nurse and midwife," whose occupation is further made clear by the presence of four small children in various positions about her.   Above we read, "she caused pain to no one, but all grieved for her after her death."[21]

For the long periods spent in sleep, the Greek child seems to have been given a very comfortable place—a cradle, of course, and one which rocked. Only one example shows a construction similar to that of the wooden cradles on rockers in common use not long ago, and here the motion, rather surprisingly, was not from side to side, but from end to end instead.[22] The usual cradle was rounded more or less on the under side, and one would imagine that it was easily set in motion by any activity on the part of the child itself.[23] It seems quite possible, too, that it could be tipped so as to roll the baby out; even so, there need have been little cause for concern, since the child obviously had not far to fall. Yet this was prevented on occasion by the use of cross straps, as we see them applied to hold a pair of small twins in position.[24]

The basket shaped cradle on the well-known Vatican vase[25] is very familiar since it is often reproduced. I have not, however, found a single other example of this type, whereas the former is frequently represented.

The occupants of these cradles vary somewhat in age; in many of them there are tiny babies, kept snug by means of cap and generous *III C* wrappings.[26] That many others are older is clear from the long hair, and their being nude;[27] for warmth they were dependent upon the thick, soft mattress or pillows upon which they rested, and, possibly, the pet now and then seen lying beside them.[28] *I B*

A most unusual method of carrying a small child occurs in one terracotta group.[29] The form of the conveyance which is seen on the mother's back suggests more than anything else a modern Greek *III D* saddle bag, though it is considerably longer. Only the head of the baby is visible, emerging from the opening at the top. Whatever other advantages this arrangement may have possessed, it does not strike one as particularly conducive to the child's comfort. Another terracotta[30] shows what is perhaps intended to be a similar article, though the curiously shaped object encasing the child, in cap and wrappings, is here rounded at the lower end. Certainly it cannot have been made to suggest an ordinary cradle.

If not asleep, a child might be seen seated in its cradle,[31] or else on a low couch,[32] playing there or observing what went on about it. Certainly it would not normally remain there long, but would quickly

III B

venture forth, on all fours, to go in search of a plaything or a playmate. On occasion, when it was desirable to control the child's activities, or to have it seated on a level with the adult, it was con-

Front. A

signed to its high chair.[33] Though differing somewhat from the modern type, these chairs seem to have been quite practical, and comfortable too, if we may draw conclusions from the attitude of the children occupying them.

Between this chair for the wee tot and that for adults, there may well have been an intermediate type. Such a form is at least suggested by several small ones of terracotta shaped somewhat like the high chair. The proportions of the foot and the upper part are practically reversed, however, and the front is entirely open instead of having merely two circular openings for the legs. Some of these chairs are without occupants,[34] but one on which a wicker design is carefully indicated has a woman with a small child seated in it.[35] The suggestion of a high chair, therefore, cannot hold for all the examples of this type.

Of course the child had to be amused somehow, and nothing was more convenient than a rattle with a nice long handle. Any one who has observed children will know that such a toy must, first of all, be durable. So the Greeks seem to have made these things of bronze, or else of wood, as is indicated in the dedication of Philokles' toys, which included a boxwood rattle, to the god Hermes.[36] There are several illustrations of some such object, held in the hand of a

IV C

small child or of the slave who attends him,[37] and the general shape brings to mind two so-called children's toys which are made of bronze.[38] Each consists of a long handle attached to the axis of a double convex disc, but they seem to lack the means of being made to rattle. On another object of similar shape,[39] this want is obviously supplied by a number of small rings inserted in holes around the edge of the disc, and in a bronze rattle of the same type from a child's grave *III E* at Olynthus, by pebbles enclosed in the disc. There is also one unusual terracotta rattle[40] with geometric decoration, shaped like a flattened round flask with a very long slender neck. For the description I am indebted to Mr. Beazley who has added the suggestion that the thing held by a child on a small oinochoe is a rattle *IV D* of this type.[41]

Curiously enough, most of the rattles which have survived the centuries are of a fragile sort; at least terracotta is not a suitable material for a toy to be put into the hand of a small child. Either these were intended for older youngsters, or else were held by the mother or nurse, and shaken to attract the child's attention. The use of the rattle by nurses to lull to rest children who do not sleep well is specifically mentioned by Pollux.[42] There is always, of course, the possibility that those which we now have are simply terracotta models made to be dedicated. Suidas, however, in his definition of κοροπλάθοι makes the statement that all sorts of little clay animals were made to amuse little children, and if animals, why not rattles? In form they are indeed interesting; we find owls, though without *IV B* feet and tail,[43] pigs with stubby snouts and holes for eyes[44] and small *IV A* tortoises.[45] Another, and not inappropriate, shape is that of a cradle complete with the figure of a child in it.[46] Even more elaborate in execution is the rattle modelled as a small boy,[47] seated on a base, *IV F* with a goose at his right side. The bird is stretching its neck in a vigorous attempt to reach some of the fruit held up, at the boy's left side, in a fold of his tiny mantle. An object not yet explained

satisfactorily is illustrated on several vases and stelai in connection
IV E   with larger children. Although generally seen in a girl's hand,[48] it
appears once in the background, resting at an angle on a shelf.[49] I
venture the suggestion that it was a rattle, somewhat similar, perhaps, in construction, to a Buddhist prayer wheel, or to a wooden
clapper from Antinoe.[50] This consists of a flat rectangular piece of
wood, cut in one with the handle, and upon each side there is tied
another rather thin square section of wood. The former objects do
not, to be sure, show details present in the latter, but there is a certain similarity in shape.

A unique rattle apparently served a double purpose, in that the
V D   pebble, or clay pellet, was inserted in a very neat feeding bottle;[51]
when this had been emptied the nurse could shake it as she lulled
the child to sleep. The feeding bottles themselves vary considerably
in detail, although they conform in general to two main types. The
V A   more slender style, suggesting a small pitcher, is open above, and the
handle is placed over the top.[52] From the standpoint of adaptability,
this form seems decidedly less practical than the second. Its length
from the spout to the top of the handle is considerable, and it is
difficult to see how it could have been tilted enough to give the child
an opportunity to absorb the contents in comfort. The second type,
even more frequent, is squat in shape, with a handle at the side. The
V C   top is occasionally left open,[53] but more often it is closed by a con-
V B   cave strainer;[54] one example rather interestingly combines the two
features, with a circular opening in the center top, and a strainer
near the edge, opposite the mouth.[55] All of these have a short spout,
set at right angles to the handle, and often carefully rounded in the
shape of a nipple.

The close tie which binds together mothers and their children is
suggested in various ways by the Greek artist. Here a child, held by
the servant or nurse, extends both arms eagerly toward the mother

who is seated, ready to receive it.[56] Often the little one is seen on her lap, lying face down[57] or held in a seated position,[58] or standing up so as to face its mother.[59] In a number of pretty groups it is not the adult's lap, but the shoulder upon which the child rests, steadied by a hand upon its ankles or knees, while its own small hand rests upon the mother's head.[60] Now and then the little figure is so completely relaxed that its drooping head makes us certain it has fallen asleep there.[61]

VI A

XL A

VII C

As soon as the child begins to show an inclination to creep, we are likely to see it crawling in the direction of some toy[62] or toward its mother; here the father stands by, looking on;[63] there the nurse anxiously extends a protecting hand.[64] When tired of moving about, it might pause to rest, with legs drawn up under its little body,[65] or, lying on its stomach, it could kick up its heels in perfect comfort.[66] If none of the grown-ups yielded to its entreating arms, extended upward,[67] even after it had attempted to climb up on the chair,[68] it might console itself by going to sleep where it was. Nothing was more natural than to sink down upon the nearest convenient object, with the head pillowed upon the arm,[69] or else to make one's small playmate a soft and cozy resting place.[70]

VII D

VI B

VII A

VII E

VII B

To make life as safe as possible for the Greek child, parents took care, evidently, to see that amulets were regularly worn. The string or cord which carried them was hung from one shoulder, and brought across the body so as to hang near the hip on the other side.[71] The number of amulets on one string varied, but there would seem to have been from three to six in most cases. It is difficult to give any accurate description of their shape, for vase painters, in general, contented themselves with merely indicating the objects. As a matter of fact, some of these may very well represent simply knots tied in the cord, as we actually do see them worn by adults on some objects from Italy.[72] Greek literature has no reference to the knot itself,

VII D

but John Chrysostom[73] mentions a scarlet thread among the articles used for prophylactic purposes. There are, however, a few vases where amulets are carefully drawn; in one instance they are shaped like an axe head and an enlarged grain of wheat.[74] On another vase[75]

XXII C

VII G they are very like the objects seen in the Cypriote sculptures;[76] the illustration will give one a much better idea of them than any description possibly could.

Not only was a cord suspended from the shoulder, but the child might be seen wearing a necklace, and one or more bracelets or anklets.

III B

VII G Some of these, also, suggest a mere cord;[77] others are obviously of metal, twisted, or wound round and round.[78] This is especially true in the case of older children, and particularly girls. One cannot help feeling that the more elaborate of these served primarily as ornaments, and only secondarily as prophylactics.

TOYS, PETS, AND GAMES

For the entertainment of the younger member of the family, who had just reached the walking stage, toys made to be moved about were undoubtedly most satisfying. One plaything of this type was an animal—a horse, surely—with arched neck and curved tail, and with four wheels instead of legs. Further, the nose was pierced, so the only thing needed was to insert the string, and the horse was ready to go.[79]

VIII B

Somewhat similar are the horses with long cylindrical bodies, carrying panniers on their backs, with two large,[80] or six smaller jars.[81] There are also very small two-wheeled carts, some of them with an opening apparently made for the insertion of a little pole.[82] The box is sometimes open at the back or front, and when this is the case the floor projects somewhat beyond the sides.[83] These carts were made either empty, or, in other cases, with from one to three figures seated in them.[84] As one goes from such simple forms to more complicated groups, there is less certainty about their having served as toys, though it is not entirely impossible. We find, for instance, a man driving a team of horses,[85] a team of mules drawing a two-wheeled cart,[86] and four-horse chariots with warrior and charioteer.[87] Because of the fact that some of them are constructed with two, three, or four movable wheels, one is unwilling to say that they were not meant to be moved about.

VIII D

VIII A
VIII C

The idea of going to market is suggested by other terracottas, not, however, on wheels. There are horses and donkeys carrying panniers of various shapes,[88] and even a dog with baskets on his back.[89] Sometimes the driver is seen seated behind the load,[90] or the

dog is allowed to ride, perched above the baskets.[91]   In other groups
the driver walks immediately behind the donkey, with a staff or
cudgel in his hand.[92]   Similar figures are an old woman riding on a
mule,[93] a donkey with a large fish tied upon its back,[94] and a seated
ape holding a two-handled jug.[95]

Small terracotta dogs,[96] horses,[97] deer,[98] cows or bulls,[99] goats,[100]

IX A rams,[101] and pigs[102] must have been general favorites. The rabbit,[103]
tortoise,[104] and cicada,[105] the lion[106] and the dolphin[107] are found, and
there occur several nibbling mice,[108] but these are made of bronze.
Terracotta birds[109] found in numbers almost everywhere are the
duck, goose, cock and dove.

If these small clay figures were a favorite means of beguiling
youngsters, live pets quite certainly were even more satisfactory.
There are a very large number of reliefs showing girls or boys holding

IX B doves, either in a very careless fashion,[110] or so as to caress them,[111]
IX C and often a small child is represented reaching for the bird held by
an adult.[112]   Many of the latter are, to be sure, too sketchy or too
much weathered to be identified with absolute certainty, but the size
suggests a dove, rather than some other bird.   In passing, brief
reference might be made to a rather large group of reliefs in which
children hold a bird of the above type so that it is nearly or completely

XV A within reach of a little dog.[113]   Since the dog is almost always in a
position which suggests its worrying the bird, one would like to
imagine that the latter represented a wooden or terracotta toy,
possibly one of the mechanical kind said to have been invented by
Archytas.[114]   Every now and then, however, the bird is held by a
wing only, or in some other equally uncomfortable position, and looks
very much alive. We are driven to the conclusion, therefore, that
children were not always urged to treat their pets with kindness, and
that the artist himself did not hesitate to portray what seems to us a
bit of unnecessary cruelty. By way of a definite example of the

difference between the viewpoint of the ancients and that of later
times, one need only refer to the popularity of the game of quail-
striking in antiquity.[115]

Another feathered friend which was popular was the goose,
with the duck a close second. Little children are sometimes seen
seated with the pet at their side,[116] and there is also the well-known
type of the small boy struggling with the goose.[117] Older girls and *X D*
boys ordinarily carry their pet ducks.[118] The goose, however, stands *X E*
near, reaching for some object, such as a bunch of grapes, in the *X A*
child's hand,[119] or else it assumes much the position that one would
expect of a pet dog, with head and neck laid against the child's body.[120]

Even more charming are the groups of children with cocks, many
of which are similar to the foregoing. Here we see a chubby hand
resting on the bird's back,[121] and elsewhere the pet, held in the arms *VII F*
of a larger boy, pecks at his ear, to the owner's great delight.[122] In an- *X B*
other pretty scene we see two boys feeding a small flock of chickens;[123] *X C*
yet one more shows two youngsters busily engaged in giving their
pet cock a ride in a small cart.[124] *XI E*

Quails there are, in a cage held on a boy's lap,[125] or perched on a
girl's hand,[126] or on the ground picking up food.[127] Another bird,
apparently a raven, is seen, again in the company of smaller children, *XXXIX B*
on the ground;[128] on a table or stool;[129] or a perch;[130] on the hand;[131] *XI ACB*
and even on a creeping child's head.[132]

Exactly what we have in the slender, long-legged birds, standing
here and there at the side of a child[133] it is difficult to say. Perhaps
they are herons, though the possibility of a stork suggests itself also.

The peacock is found a number of times, beside the figure of *XI D*
Eros or of a boy.[134] As one can hardly assume that it was found as a
pet, except on rare occasions, it is better, perhaps, to attribute these
groups to a certain freedom of imagination on the artist's part. Going a little further, one might mention other fanciful scenes, such as

XI F children or Erotes riding on cocks,[135] geese,[136] or even dolphins,[137] and lions.[138] Similarly there are teams of cocks,[139] geese,[140] and peacocks,[141] drawing carts in which children ride.

Of all the domestic animals, dogs were manifestly the greatest favorites. They are represented in a variety of characteristic attitudes, scampering along before or behind the children,[142] standing
XXVI B on their hind legs, begging for something,[143] licking the face of the
XII BC baby which embraces them,[144] or sitting patiently near the chair while the small master or mistress is otherwise occupied.[145] There
XIII A are teams of dogs, with elaborate harness, drawing carts in which children are seated,[146] and many a patient pet submits to being ridden by the little boy seated astride its back.[147] These dogs often wear
XXIX D collars, just as ours do today, and rather frequently there is suspended from the collar what looks exactly like a tiny bell.[148]

Numerous parallels to the above groups are found also among the illustrations of other animals. The small pig which is carried by a girl,[149] for example, may not be a pet at all, but destined for sacrifice.
XII D On the other hand, a considerable number of small children are
XII E found riding on larger pigs.[150] The cow or ox feeds from a child's
XII A hand,[151] or carries him about;[152] rams and goats are ridden[153] and
XIII C fed,[154] and the latter appear a number of times hitched to carts, either single[155] or in teams.[156]

There are varying illustrations of boys riding horses. We see a
XIV B man standing so as to help a boy mount,[157] elsewhere a lad stands upright on his horse's back,[158] and still another vase shows the horse about to leap over some object lying in its path, while the boy holds the reins tight.[159] Sometimes there is a whip with double lash in the rider's hand,[160] and in a few cases we see a sort of pad, for his comfort, on the back of the horse.[161]

XIV D Deer are found rather more frequently than one would expect,
XIII BD petted,[162] ridden,[163] or drawing carts on which children ride.[164] The

hare or rabbit makes its appearance in a number of ways. When
held up by the front paws only[165] we would prefer to think it one
caught in the hunt, rather than a pet thus dealt with.   An older girl
who holds a little rabbit in the "apron" of her chiton is truly much   *XIV E*
more kind;[166] boys, too, are seen elsewhere, stroking the little animal   *XIV F*
as it sits on a table.[167]   One pet hare is observed just in the act of   *XIII E*
leaping over a boy's small cart,[168] and one delightful little painting
shows a boy with hands resting on his knees, stooping toward a hare   *XIII F*
which is seated on its hind legs and looks up at him.[169]

A certain lack of feeling, or sympathy, for animals, which is
noticeable from time to time is again to be seen in the case of a girl
who is holding up a tortoise by means of a string tied to one leg.[170]   *XV C*
Other groups show us children either simply looking at a tortoise,[171]
or with the hand upon its back,[172] or with a foot resting upon it.[173]

One isolated example will conclude this rather long list of pets,
namely, a mouse.[174]   A boy or youth is seen seated with a large round   *XIV AC*
dish, obviously containing some food, on his lap.   His hands rest on
the sides of the bowl, and on the edge, on a sort of small handle, the
mouse is comfortably seated.

Since occasional references have already been made to carts, a
brief discussion will not be out of place here.   Most of them are
drawn in profile, so it is not easy to decide in all cases just what is
represented.   As a matter of fact, the term has been applied to a
large number of objects which are not really carts at all, but a simpler
form of plaything, made with a single wheel,[175] or possibly a pair of   *XI A*
them, set rather close together.[176]   By means of the long pole attached   *XV A*
the child then pushed the toy about.   One boy is seen raising such an
object high in one hand,[177] and so we feel more certain that it was
simple and light in weight.   Some of these have a cross-bar,[178] serving
as a handle, fastened near the front end of the pole, while in others
there is no handle to be seen.

Of the carts proper, the smallest looks like a simple little platform, more or less raised above the wheels. Such is the form of the two on which children have set small jugs,[179] and a somewhat larger one carries a boy's pet hare.[180] The latter cart is drawn so as to suggest a complete box, rather than a flat surface only, but the position of the hare, on top, and not in it, would seem to determine the

XV D   form. Some illustrations, however, do show a box very clearly.[181]

Front. B   Still other types are best described by the terms chariot and go-cart. In the latter the figure is seated, naturally, since there is a support at the back, and sometimes at the sides too.[182] In the former the child, in a kneeling or standing position, generally, holds fast to the rail.[183] Occasionally this little chariot is drawn by children,[184] but

XIII C   more frequently by animals of one sort or another.[185] Anyte of Tegea describes so well this form of childish amusement that it seems worth while to add here a complete translation of the poem.[186]

"The children, billy goat, have put purple reins on you, and a muzzle on your bearded face; and they train you to race, like horses, round the temple of the god, that you may draw them as they rejoice in their childish play."

In the list of playthings which, we would suppose, had been designed particularly for girls, the doll stands first. We have a number of reliefs showing us girls or women actually holding them in their hands. They are of various types, either seated[187] or upright,[188] and

XV B   I am inclined to think that two of these[189] are suspended from a loop or string held in the hand.

While many of these dolls must have been dressed, as dolls are now, only one has been found to give any proof of the fact; it wears a chiton, exactly as does the small girl who holds it in her hand.[190]

Though dolls were made of other materials such as bone and wood, by far the largest number which have come down to us are of

XVI C   terracotta. The well-known Boeotian bell-shaped "doll" hardly leads one to believe that it was actually used as a toy,[191] but the other kinds certainly were. In spite of variations of detail, they conform rather closely to several main types.

There is the flat figure, with high headdress or cap, like that of the Greek priest (*pappas*) of today, with arms and legs attached at the shoulders and hips respectively.[192] Both this type and other jointed figures were frequently made with crotala or clappers in the hands.   *XVI B*

A smaller number of dolls, best represented by a little one of bone, wear a short skirt reaching to the knees; the joint, then, comes just below.[193] This costume suggests that worn by the professional dancing girls, and we are reminded also, in this connection, of the puppets, νευρόσπαστα, mentioned by Xenophon.[194]

A third class shows the body well rounded and modeled with   *XVI A* greater care, and the head, with hair high at the back, frequently has a kerchief or band fastened about it. If the figures are complete, the legs are generally attached at the knee,[195] instead of higher up.   *X E* A number of these, however, are made with the legs ending at the   *XVI D* knees, and with only a part of the upper arm.[196]

Again, the doll is seated, with arms jointed at the shoulder, but with legs which are immovable.[197] One would be more inclined to   *XVI E* classify these last as purely votive offerings, were it not for the additional information we have regarding one which was found in a tomb near Athens.[198] This one is seated in a high-backed chair; in her hand is an ivory dove, and beside her a tiny onos or knee protector, used in spinning or carding, a pair of shoes, and a lebes gamikos or marriage bowl. The British Museum authorities suggest that this small lebes indicated the tomb of a newly wedded bride;[199] on the other hand, it is not altogether impossible to imagine that it, or some of the other similar ones,[200] were used by children for dolls' weddings.   *XVII D*

Other small dishes which may have been toys are in the form of a hydria (water jar),[201] pyxis (toilet box),[202] oinochoe (wine pitcher),[203] and lekythos (oil flask).[204] There are numerous tiny jars and pots of varying shapes,[205] baskets with high handles,[206] and one model of a sort of range or fire pot, with cooking vessel in it.[207] A pretty little terracotta oven, with an opening at the lower right side for the fire, is open in front so that one is able to see a large number of small round cakes within.[208] Still other utensils are a candelabrum,[209] a ladle,[210] and a strainer with long handle.[211] Small trays and baskets

XVII B   filled with fruit, bread, etc. are found now and then, but they are more likely to have been offerings of a religious nature.[212]

Among the articles of furniture we have tables, with both round

XVII A   and rectangular tops. The former regularly have three legs,[213] the latter normally four,[214] though one was made with only three, namely two at the corners of one end, with the third in the middle of the other end.[215] There are chairs with arms and high backs,[216] couches

XVII C   complete with cushions,[217] and a low, rectangular stool.[218] A miniature stone chest may have been a welcome toy,[219] and there is one cradle large enough to have accommodated some little girl's doll.[220] A terracotta model of a temple is more likely to have served a religious purpose than to have been a plaything, but the latter is at least a possibility.[221]

While I have found no representation of a mask actually worn

XVIII C   by a child, one sees them held in the hand rather frequently.[222] One would infer, therefore, that children took pleasure in playing with them, and it seems quite natural that they should. There is one small

XVIII D   boy, however, who appears to have been filled with terror by a large mask; he is looking back at it even as he runs away, and on the ground we see a jug which he may have put down in his haste to escape.[223]

An interesting plaything which brings to mind the mechanical wooden toys made at the present time in Russia, is a terracotta in the form of a woman with kneading trough before her. There are movable joints in the arms and at the hips, so that she could be made to do her work very satisfactorily.[224] Of the same type, apparently, is the figure of a woman, in Leyden, occupied in grinding.[225]

There seems little doubt that the whipping top was a plaything which provided enjoyment for many. As one would expect, because of the skill required for spinning, it was popular chiefly with the older children. Other illustrations prove that even adults did not despise the toy. Its shape was either simply that of a cone, with sides slightly curved,[226] or else it was cylindrical, with a short cone-shaped *XVIII B* base.[227] Many are made of terracotta, but a number of bronze have been found also.[228] The height of the known examples varies from about two and one-half, to eight or nine inches. The manner in which they were kept in motion by means of a whip is clear from a number of illustrations showing boys and girls, or adults, with a lash *XVIII A* in the hand, intent upon the spinning top.[229]

For the older boys, the hoop seems to have been a parallel to the little boy's wheel, since only one example of the former in the hand of a small child has been found.[230] One hoop is so drawn as to suggest its having been made in three sections, probably of wood accordingly, with some binding at each joint;[231] another vase painting shows a *XX D* hoop thus joined in one place only.[232] There are a number of illustrations of boys actually rolling their hoops,[233] as well as of boys[234] and one girl[235] where the toy is simply held in the hand. The stick used *XX A* seems generally to have been quite short, but there is some variety. A lively scene shows us not only the boy running and holding his *XX D* hoop, but his small dog also, apparently enjoying the chase.[236] A hoop put to another purpose is that held by a kneeling girl and boy, while their little dog leaps through it.[237]

With hoops and tops we are very likely to associate marbles or jackstones, and the Greek parallel is not hard to find. Of their knucklebones or astragals which have come down to us some are the bones themselves[238] and others are made of metal and stone.[239] The game of five-stones, played with astragals or pebbles, corresponds to our own method of playing jackstones; they are thrown up and caught on the back of the hand. If any fall to the ground they must be retrieved by the same hand without losing those already caught. We *XIX D* find several pairs of girls[240] facing each other in a kneeling position *XIX B* with the right hand up, and, while details are lacking, what we do see agrees with the description given by Pollux,[241] even corroborating his statement that five-stones is, above all, a woman's game. One *XIX C* other terracotta group shows the girls with their hands full, ready for a throw, apparently.[242] Since one such player holds in her left hand *XIX A* an elongated purse or bag,[243] often carried by children in the terracottas,[244] it is quite possible that it served as a bag for the objects, much as the marble bag of today. The lad Konnaros, mentioned in the *Anthology*,[245] who received eighty astragals as a prize for writing, certainly had need of some such container.

Another form of the game is illustrated in a terracotta group of three girls.[246] They are gathered around a circle, with diameter indicated, marked on the ground, and within the circle lie three astragals. We know from Pollux[247] that the object in $\epsilon is\ \ddot{\omega}\mu\iota\lambda\lambda a\nu$ was to prevent the astragals from falling outside. Here the line drawn through the circle probably made the game more difficult. For other games of this type which we find named in literature, such as playing "odd and even" with astragals,[248] the Greek artist has left us nothing except possibly the dice with which the boys played.[249]

Balls were of interest to every period of life, from that of the babies which awkwardly clutch them[250] or crawl after them,[251] to that of adults. We often see girls and boys playing in exactly the same fashion. If there is only one player, he may be standing[252] or kneeling[253] or comfortably seated,[254] and it is not unusual to see one ball

for each hand.[255]   Some vase fragments show one girl throwing a ball
to be caught by another, and there are indications of a third girl for
the group.[256]

Something like a wicket is found in three illustrations, one of
girls,[257] the others of boys.[258] In each, a ball is held high in one player's   *XX E*
right hand, while the opposite player behind the wicket stoops and
extends both hands, ready to catch the ball.

A ball game curious to us is several times repeated with only
slight modifications. The plan seems to have been to have a ball
thrown by one person, in the direction of one,[259] two,[260] or even three   *XX B*
players,[261] all seated on the shoulders of others. In nearly every
instance the carriers' hands rest on their knees, while the riders extend
theirs to catch the ball. In another form of the game, one boy who is
carried throws the ball to a number of others who stand on the
ground.[262] The winner then presumably mounted upon the shoulders
of the boy who threw the ball, as the game is still played in northern
Greece in modern times.[263]

The game of ephedrismos has given rise to much discussion and
there are some who have tried to distinguish sharply between this
and the game spoken of as ἐν κοτύλῃ. In view of the numerous
variations which any well-known game may undergo at any time, it is
wiser, no doubt, to agree with those who suggest that the two are
practically alike. A vase painting[264] shows us one stage of the former
as described by Pollux;[265] the boy who failed to strike the barrier with
the ball is forced to carry the winner on his back. In addition he must
find the barrier while blindfolded. There is no serious objection to our
thinking of the numerous terracotta groups of girls[266] as showing the   *XX C*
same penalty, even though they are not blindfolded by having the
winner's hands over their eyes. The mere task of carrying a playmate
for a given distance in this position is punishment enough; it must

have been very difficult to keep the hands clasped behind one's back, with a weight resting on the arm.

It seems worth while to refer here to two well-known reliefs in Athens. Although both of them show youths, rather than boys, at *XXI A*   play, the group of ball players[267] has certain parallels in the preceding paragraphs. The second relief is more interesting, perhaps, because *XXI B*   it is the more unusual—the so-called hockey base.[268] One can safely state that children everywhere are certain to imitate the things they see done by older people; therefore we may add the suggestion that the little boys at times must have instituted hockey games of their own.

Certain other illustrations offer less difficulty than some of the foregoing since we have no need to consult literary passages for their interpretation. Almost any child likes to ride on the foot of an adult, *XXII A*   and Greek children must have enjoyed this fun also. Our illustrations are of Eros, to be sure, but clearly the suggestion was taken from real *XXII E*   life.[269] Then, too, there is the lad riding on a stick, with whip and reins conspicuous enough to make the meaning clear.[270] One is reminded at once of Plutarch's story about King Agesilaus who was discovered by one of his friends astride a reed, playing horse with his children.[271]

Jumping the rope is without much doubt the occupation of a girl on a small stele,[272] although I have not seen it thus explained by any one else. The girl's arms are in about the same position as those of a satyr in bronze skipping the rope.[273] The rope was restored in the latter case, I understand, while the former shows all except a little at the top, where the stele is broken.

The see-saw was in use, and in spite of the fact that our two *XXIII B*   illustrations are those of very large girls or women, we may assume that children, too, amused themselves in this fashion.[274] The two satyrs kneeling at opposite ends of a board[275] are apparently playing something else, for we observe the board is short enough to allow one satyr to grasp the wrists of the other. This board is balanced on a small triangular support and it seems more likely that it was rotated rapidly instead of being moved up and down.

As for swings, the simpler form is that consisting of a rope only,[276] *XXIII A* apparently without even the small board which we often use as a seat in our swings today. The other more elaborate form is a four-legged stool or chair suspended by means of cords or ropes.[277] In each illustration some one stands behind to push the person sitting in the swing.

The kite is known through only one illustration where it is distinctly drawn in the form of a triangle, with the string attached at the center of the base.[278]

Another toy is held in a way to suggest what I have often seen played with even such things as a large coat button. There must be two openings so that the string can be drawn through from one side and brought back again through the second hole; then the ends are best knotted together securely. The loop at either end is held with the hand, or only a finger, and when the string is alternately drawn tight and again slackened, the disc whirls first in one direction, then back in the other, as the string is wound up and again unwound. When made to twirl rapidly the button or disc produces a pleasant humming noise. In the illustrations, objects of this kind appear in the hands of women *XXII C* and Erotes rather frequently.[279] To such the term "magic wheel" is undoubtedly applicable; at the same time, it would be rather strange if children had not amused themselves with such a plaything also.

The boy who stands holding in his right hand a string with something round at the end[280] is generally supposed to be playing with a sort of spool such as is still used today. When the spool is released from the fingers the string unwinds, and if properly managed the spool will return a number of times, winding up the string as it comes. It hardly seems possible to accept seriously the suggestion that the terracotta bobbins[281] could be used thus; certainly they were too fragile. If, however, they were made of other material for the use of the children, or with different proportions, so as to strengthen the core, they might have proved very entertaining. Another possible explanation is that the object represents the flat disc of leather attached to a string which modern children call a sucker. The leather is soaked and pressed tight to a stone or other object which, held fast by suction, can then be lifted.[282]

A game evidently similar to that called "morra" by the Italians at the present time is illustrated in several places. Two players, seated facing each other, hold up, at the same time, a certain number of fingers of the right hand. The one who first calls the total number correctly wins. Most of the illustrations found differ from the modern form of the game, however, in that the two players hold between them, with their left hands, a staff. In several cases one player's hand is in such a position that it seems to be measuring off a part of

XXII B the staff,[283] and twice we see a small winged figure flying with a wreath to the girl whose hand is at the end.[284] The usual explanation is that the final winner in the game is the one who first counts off his half of the staff, on the assumption that each correct guess allows a given space on it.

A butterfly hunt is found on a small vase where we see a boy with body eagerly stretched forward, going as fast as his legs can carry him. The butterfly just beyond his reach is painted in a bluish glaze.[285]

Fishing is a pastime twice found. In one case[286] the boy is again Eros, who is assisting his mother Aphrodite to draw in a fish which

XX F has taken the hook. In the second scene[287] a boy alone is seated on the rocky shore, with a small basket in his left hand. The right holds the fishing pole, and one of the six fish we see in the water below seems about to bite. Farther out there is an interesting object suggesting a lobster pot, and under the shadow of a rock reposes an octopus, an article of food still prized by the Greeks of today.

ATHLETIC EXERCISES

Regular training in athletics and participation in contests are generally associated with the ephebes, but formal contests for boys were an established feature at Olympia and elsewhere. On a vase to which reference has already been made in connection with the top and ball,[288] there are further a boy in the act of throwing the discus and two others engaged in wrestling. The trainer stands near them, resting on his staff as he looks on. It is evidently the winner in some contest of this type whom we see on another vase,[289] standing between two men of whom one is about to place a wreath upon his head.

Informal scenes of play, on the other hand, are more frequently found. A boy[290] with arms extended is preparing to jump over a low stele or post standing before him. Apparently there are no jumping weights in his hands, and he is obviously not practicing the ordinary broad jump of the athlete. Pairs of wrestlers appear, either as small boys or Erotes.[291] In some of these groups it is quite clear, however, that they are merely quarreling, over a bird, for instance,[292] and it is possible that none of them should be spoken of as wrestlers.

XXIII C

We see girls as would-be jugglers,[293] balancing a stick on the finger. There is a little boy turning a somersault,[294] and another with acrobatic tendencies stands on his hands.[295] Possibly the dish seen on the ground, just beyond his nose, is used also in the performance. One little vase[296] has an unusual picture of a boy in the act of getting up on a table; one foot is up on the edge, and his right hand is extended to help keep his balance. An interesting suggestion is that the boy is preparing to give an exhibition of his skill—possibly a dance after the manner of Hippokleides in Herodotus' story.[297]

XXIV C

XXIV B

Violent exercise was likely to be followed by a bath; doubtless this is suggested by the jar standing beside a boy, as well as by the strigil he holds in his hand.[298] Where the boy represented is still rather small,[299] the strigil and oil flask are carried by the slave who attends

XXIV A   him. Much more unusual is the fountain scene[300] where some women are gathered to fill jars and one of the spouts has been appropriated by a boy who is crouched under the stream of water, obviously enjoying his shower bath. The laver with its high foot is shown to good

XXIV D   advantage in several drawings. In one[301] we see a small boy, just tall enough to get his arms over the edge, in another[302] it is an older girl, while on a gem[303] a girl, though it may be a woman, is washing her hair as she bends over the laver.

SACRIFICE AND FESTIVALS

It seems reasonable to assume that Greek children participated in sacrifices although we do not have much definite evidence. In each of the illustrations found the child is, as one would expect, rather a large one. We have a boy[304] about to pour a libation, with oinochoe in his right hand and a sort of cup in the left. A thymiaterion or incense burner occupies the center of another picture[305] and the boys who stand on either side have wreaths of leaves on their heads. Among the figures on votive reliefs[306] there is sometimes that of a boy standing near an altar who carries a tray or shallow basket filled with offerings. A vase painting[307] shows a boy, going to sacrifice, with a tray supported on his left hand, while with his right he is carrying a pig, held by its hind leg. There have been found, also, in a sanctuary, terracotta figures of boys[308] each holding a small pig in front of the breast, and these suggest that the boys carrying goats on their shoulders[309] in a manner similar to that of the well-known "Moschophorus," have to do with sacrifice also.

There is a tendency on the part of some modern writers to associate the toy jugs which are found in such numbers with the Festival of the Pitchers or Χόες. This was the name given to the second day of the Anthesteria because, so Athenaeus states,[310] the men at Athens took part in a drinking contest on that occasion. A measure of wine was placed before each, and he who first drained it received a cake as his prize. The wreaths with which the men had adorned themselves were then placed about the jugs.

In Philostratus[311] we are told that at Athens the children between two and three years of age were adorned with wreaths of flowers

XXV D

XXV E

in the month Anthesterion. We do not learn, however, on what days
of the month this occurred.

    With the above statements in mind it seems quite natural to
connect the children's jugs with this festival, but in literature there is
no proof of the fact. On many of them we do see children with jugs in
their hands,[312] or else walking or crawling toward a low table with
jugs and fruit.[313] Sometimes the children wear wreaths,[314] sometimes
there is a small wreath about the neck of the jug.[315] At other times
we see the attention of the youngsters divided between jugs and a
large flat round cake,[316] or else there is an object which may be a
twisted roll.[317] This varies considerably in size, but possibly we
should not consider proportions of these objects too seriously when
they appear in drawings which are obviously sketchy. In general
there is a festive air about many of the small pictures, and the rather
frequent addition of a tiny cart[318] to the objects already named suggests that the artist had in mind an occasion for gifts. There occur
other vase paintings which show, also, a tray with grapes or other
things upon it, carried toward a table.[319] Beside another table[320]
stands a child pouring something from a pitcher, while his playmate is
bringing a large platter. Obviously the children are here preparing to
celebrate a feast of some kind. As suggested before, we can only
conjecture regarding details in many cases; the drawings are frequently made in so careless a fashion that the attempt to interpret
only tantalizes one.

    Processions of children are extremely charming. One of these[321]
is headed by a small dog with a jug suspended around his neck. He is
followed by a team of boys drawing a cart in which is seated another
boy with a lyre on his knees. A rather pretentious Dionysiac pro-
cession[322] consists of Dionysus himself, with kantharos and wand,
riding in a covered wagon, with five individuals following behind. A
group of four revellers[323] carrying wreathed jugs is guided by a blazing

XXV A

XXV B

XXVI A

IV E

XXV C

Front. C

XXVI D

XXVI F

torch in the hands of the first child; one of those who follow obviously needs the support which his companion is lending him. A Bacchic revel[324] is made livelier by the sound of a tympanum or tambourine, and the presence of a little dog which is taking an active part. Still another group[325] is celebrating with flutes, a tympanum and the light of a torch; here a jug standing on the ground between two of the boys prompts the suggestion that they may be marching or dancing about it. A child with a torch,[326] and a pet goose walking along at the side, looks away to one side as though waiting for others to join it. In the drawings where we see a child running with a blazing torch[327] we can easily believe that there is a torch race in progress.

XXVI C

Sometimes a childish frolic centers about a herm. One of our terracotta groups consists of two children[328] and what looks like a figure of Priapus; the one child stands in front reaching up, while the other sits on the herm's left shoulder grasping his beard with one hand. In another group there are four children,[329] sitting up on the herm or clinging to it, and their playmate, a pet goat, is lying quietly at the base.

XXVI E

SCHOOL

In addition to training in music, the regular Greek curriculum contained, apparently, only reading, writing, and a certain amount of arithmetic. We find some very interesting things here, beginning with a piece of marble upon which the alphabet was inscribed.[330] A phonic chart on a fragment of pottery has all the letters in a column combined with each of the vowels in turn.[331] On a wooden writing tablet with iron handle is written in ink a reading exercise from the first book of the Iliad.[332] Wax tablets were generally made as are our slates, with a thin coating of wax over the central part.[333] In Herondas[334] we read of an exasperated mother who laboriously renewed this wax every month for her intractable son. The characters were then scratched in this surface by means of a stylus, an instrument pointed at one end, but with the other flat, so as to enable the writer to correct errors by spreading the wax again. Two good examples are made of ivory[335] and of bronze,[336] each a little over five inches in length. Some of the tablets are blank,[337] while one[338] has a line of Greek, copied twice below by the pupil. On another[339] appear some multiplication tables including the twos and threes through "times ten." The letters of the alphabet are used in order, to designate the numbers, with the old digamma representing six.

XXVII

Nor are illustrations of children at these tasks lacking. There are many showing the old paidagogos, or slave attendant, leading his small charge,[340] and we assume that the two are on their way to school. Although it is generally stated that girls did not attend school, there are certain exceptions to be mentioned here. An inscription from Teos[341] records the fact that provision was made for three teachers to

XXVIII D

give instruction to the girls there as well as to the boys. Another interesting thing is a fifth century vase painting[342] showing a girl, rather large, led by a woman who is pointing the way. That they are going to school is apparent from the tablet the girl carries, and also from the reluctance with which she goes. A rather chubby little girl in terracotta[343] stands holding her tablet in the right hand, and a purse perhaps containing her astragals in the left.

XXIX B

XXVIII A

In company with the old schoolmaster who is seated, we find small boys reading from the scroll they hold in their hands[344] or which rests upon a sort of reading stand.[345] At other times a folding tablet is laid upon the teacher's knees,[346] and the pupil is either reading or observing what the schoolmaster is writing there. In one case[347] the boy is seated also, and himself holds the tablet upon which the teacher's finger rests.

XXVIII E
XXVIII C
XXVIII B

Both girls and boys appear alone, simply carrying their tablets[348] or holding them on their knees,[349] with a stylus held in the right hand. Among the more unusual illustrations is a pair of twins[350] seated side by side, apparently learning their a-b-c's from the tablet they are holding. An older boy[351] sits with his chin resting on his right hand, while his left holds one end of the scroll in whose contents he is so deeply absorbed. A girl Abeita[352] who, as we learn from the inscription, died at the age of ten years and two months, is reading so industriously from a roll that even her pet dog is neglected. Notice also the reading stand which the artist has included in the relief.

XXX C
XXX A

XXIX D

One vase[353] shows us a group of boys perhaps playing school. One carries a tablet, and two have rolls in their hands. Two others holding staves are paidagogoi apparently, and one seated figure holding out his hand for the boy's roll is then the schoolmaster.

XXIX A

In two illustrations[354] where the master holds a scroll, the boy standing before him is apparently reciting some part of its contents which he has been committing to memory. In another group[355] the

XXXI A

XXXI B   boy is about to have a writing exercise corrected, perhaps, for he is watching the seated man who holds a stylus and an open triptych instead of the usual diptych. The old paidagogos with his staff sits near them while he waits for the boy.

Music lessons are found in a variety of illustrations. Where the teacher simply uses his right hand for directions of some sort,[356] it is not clear whether the position of the pupil's head indicates that he is singing, or whether he is only delivering a bit of oratory. Where the teacher plays the flutes, we are certain, however, that they provide the accompaniment to the boy's song.[357] Evidently it was not always necessary to sing from memory, for there are boys with scrolls in their *XXIX C*   hands, singing to the music of the lyre[358] as well as of the flute.[359] *XXXI B*   In another scene[360] the boy who is listening to his teacher's flute-playing stands facing him; on the wall we see suspended a roll, a *XXXI A*   diptych, and a lyre. Another music pupil[361] being trained to play the lyre is seated on a stool, bending anxiously over his instrument; the master and he, it appears, are playing together.

While literature offers us numerous references to the training of girls in the domestic arts, there is very little concerning school work for them. Archaeology, on the other hand, provides illustrations of girls reading and writing, or going to school, while we look in vain for *XXXII D*   domestic education. One rather crude terracotta[362] shows a girl standing beside her mother who is busy cooking; the child may be making serious observations, but she may be simply looking on, or begging for a taste, as children like to do. Of spinning, too, I have found little evidence in illustrations; the distaff which was noted in two vase paintings[363] is held not by a girl, but by a boy, apparently, in each case.

In a small group of terracottas[364] there appears a little boy, *XXXII B*   seated on the shoulder of an older male figure. While not perfectly clear, it seems that we have represented in these a slave or paidogogos

with the child which he is taking somewhere, or escorting back home
again.   Sometimes there is a basket hung on the man's arm, and there
is regularly another object which is, without much question, a lantern
of cylindrical form.   A curious object found in the right hand of a
youthful figure[365] has at times been called a lantern also, though it is   *XXXII A*
quite different in shape from any of the extant examples or representa-
tions of a Greek lantern.   Perhaps it was simply for want of a better
name—at any rate, it still awaits a satisfactory explanation.

MUSIC AND DANCING

Of the musical instruments which we meet in connection with children, the tympanum, as well as the flute, has already been mentioned. The former is found also in several terracottas, possibly, held

XXXII C

in a girl's right hand;[366] one cannot, however, feel certain about these particular objects. The lyre appears rather frequently, as it does among adults also. Either a boy is seen leaning upon it,[367] or resting it upon a pillar,[368] or about to place it upon a table.[369] We even find a small boy, with his lyre, seated upon a horse.[370] A very pretty scene is found on a vase where a little boy, walking as he plays, is preceded by his dog and followed by a pet bird.[371]

Although dancing generally implies music of some sort, there are a number of illustrations where no instruments are in evidence. We find a small boy alone[372] between an altar and a jug, while another[373] is flanked by jug and toy cart. Possibly the joy they feel because of these gifts is their sole inspiration. A girl alone[374] holds her chiton

XXX B

out at the sides as she moves, while two older girls,[375] whose garments show the sweep of the dance, hold out their hands so that they touch lightly. Three boys[376] form a merry group as they keep time with the tympanum which we see one of them beating.

Formal instruction in dancing is found also, the pupils in each case being girls. They wear chitons reaching to the knees, and their hair is short or simply gathered loosely at the back. In one illustration[377] the girl has her arms out, as though to balance herself, while the

XXXIII A
XXXIII B

others[378] have their arms bent so that their hands seem to rest on the hips. The music generally is that of the flute, but in one case[379] there is a stringed instrument suspended on the wall, while the woman simply gives directions with her right hand to the two girls before her.

PUNISHMENT

Corporal punishment seems to have been administered generally by means of a sandal; at least this is true in the matter of home discipline. In three cases the offender is Eros, looking as uncomfortable as any child could. His mother has him on her lap in one illustration[380] and in another[381] he is kneeling, apparently begging for indulgence, while she threatens as she stands near him. In the third[382] he is represented as a larger boy, standing with back turned toward Aphrodite, and extending suppliant hands, for delivery from the uplifted sandal, to the woman who stands in front. The two remaining illustrations show us situations which are somewhat different. In the one case[383] a little boy has already been punished, showing five distinct marks of the sandal on his body. In the other,[384] a woman who is seated holds the sandal, just removed from her foot, in her right hand; her left hand grasps firmly the wrists of a boy who faces her and who is apparently tugging violently in the vain hope of escaping the ordeal.

A gem of Graeco-Roman date[385] suggests that another method prevailed in the schools, for here the culprit is receiving a whipping from one of the two boys, apparently school-mates, who hold him up in the air meanwhile. Exactly the same situation is suggested by the words of the schoolmaster in Herondas[386] who calls out, "Here! Where's Euthies, where's Kokkalos, where's Phillos? Take this boy up on your shoulders at once, will you?"

XXXIV B

XXXIV A

COSTUME

The clothing used for infants has already been discussed as fully as our evidence will permit. For the period following infancy, however, a number of observations should be added, to qualify the statement that the child was generally nude. Children carried in the arms of the mother or nurse are usually represented without a garment,[387] and those which creep about always are.[388] In every case where it is possible to determine the child's sex, it proves to be a boy. Where little girls are found on toy vases they wear a chiton, or tunic, or the hair is high.[389] In the grave reliefs, where we often see small children, it is clear that even the smallest girl is dressed in a long chiton.[390] All of this points to the conclusion that while boys were often allowed to creep or run about unhampered, girls of all ages wore the chiton. The presence of such a garment on the figure of the baby,[391] lying on the lap of its nurse, distinguishes it, therefore, as a little girl from the more numerous baby boys.

The small cloak, clasped on the right shoulder, as mentioned before, is found here and there.[392] Another wrap, seen rather infrequently, is a long cape reaching nearly to the feet, with a pointed hood attached.[393] When dressed in this sort of garment, only the wearer's face and feet are visible. It seems sometimes to have been made with only an opening cut for the face, so as to slip on over the head; in other cases we see the overlapping edges of the cape in front. In some instances the cloak is a short one, but covers the head in similar fashion.[394]

The chiton worn by older boys reaches only to the knees or a little below. It is often ungirded,[395] but, where a girdle is occasionally

worn, it is placed low over the hips.[396]   The sleeve, if present at all, is   *XIV D*
always very short; it is not shaped, but is formed by the extension of   *XXXV D*
the shoulder seam over the upper arm.   As suggested before, the girl
apparently wears a full-length chiton always.   The sleeve, when pres-
sent, varies in length, sometimes reaching nearly to the elbow, with a   *IX C*
row of small clasps or buttons to hold together the edges of the front
and back.[397]   The girdle is worn in a variety of ways.   It may be simply
tied around at the waist line or a little higher.[398]   Often there is an   *XIV E*
additional crossing of the cord in front, after bringing the ends down
from the shoulders.[399]   Or, instead of crossing the two cords over the
breast, they may be simply carried back again under each arm.[400]   *X E*
Where the cord is crossed, we often see a sort of large brooch, and this   *XXXVI B*
frequently appears on the shoulders as well.[401]   If two chitons are   *XXXVI A*
worn, the one underneath, of finer material, has sleeves, while the
heavier one, worn over it, is without.[402]

The himation or mantle is worn by both girls and boys, and for
the latter it is, at times, the sole garment.   A frequent arrangement
common to both sexes is to bring the himation back over the left   *Front. B*
shoulder and arm, then down around the right hip, and back again to   *XXXVIII A*
the left side, where the ends are held on the arm and hand.[403]   Thus
the right shoulder and arm are left free for action.   Again, it may be   *XXXVIII D*
carried over the right shoulder as it is brought around from the back,
and so the entire body is protected.   Such an arrangement[404] is often
seen worn by even the smallest lads who are being led to school by
their paidagogoi.   A girl is occasionally seen imitating her mother by
wearing the himation so as to cover even the head,[405] but this occurs
only rarely. What one would normally expect active children to do with
such a garment, when not absolutely necessary for warmth, actually
was often done.   One sees it many times simply carried over the left
shoulder,[406] or twisted once around the lower arm,[407] where it was cer-   *XXXII C*
tainly less of an impediment than when worn in the approved fashion.

The short cloak or chlamys which was fastened upon the right shoulder was ordinarily the garment of the ephebe. Where the petasos, or broad-brimmed hat, is worn with it, the figure is almost certainly that of a youth about eighteen years of age.[408] In some cases, *XIV F*   however, and especially in combination with a small hat, a cloak of the same general type, with brooch on the right shoulder, is worn by boys also.[409]

In the arrangement of the hair we find striking similarities; it is, in fact, often impossible to distinguish between girls and boys unless we consider their dress also. A favorite method, to judge from the frequency with which it occurred, was to part the hair in the middle, and to allow it to hang free on both sides of the face;[410] it usually has *XXXVII B*   the appearance of being curly, so it is difficult to decide about the length, but it was almost certainly kept trimmed. Often a bit of the hair on top of the head was arranged otherwise; the suggestion that this originated because of the desire to have a lock of uncut hair for consecration is quite plausible. The disposition of the lock varies; *X D*   some children have a small knot or puff immediately over the fore-*XIX A*   head;[411] in other cases it looks like an elaborate puff farther back on *XXXII C*   the head;[412] still others have it arranged along the line of parting.[413] Sometimes this would seem to be a single or double twist, but where *XXII D*   we have more careful work it unquestionably represents a braid.

XIX B   The long hair of older girls is often parted, brushed back, and *XIX D*   clasped behind so that it hangs loosely down the back.[414] Frequently we see it fastened in a knot or coil behind,[415] exactly as it was worn by women also. How to interpret the arrangement[416] of which the appearance is so well described by the term "melonen-frisur" is rather a question. One finds it somewhat difficult to believe that girls and women actually had their hair parted into so many longitudinal sections, and that each little section was arranged in a twist extending back so that the ends were used to form the usual knot. It is much easier to suppose that we have in these examples merely a convention of the artist to represent wavy hair. Very infrequently girls, and even the small boys sometimes, have the hair arranged in one or two braids laid around the head;[417] in the case of the latter, it may have been done to imitate their older athlete brothers, among whom the arrangement is common.

XXXVII A

A band, sometimes narrow, often rather wide, was worn by many of the children whose hair was loose, perhaps to help in keeping it back from the face. It resembles in many cases a simple cord,[418] in others it is the stephane,[419] rather wide all around, but in front widening still more so as to form a point at the upper edge. What its thickness was we can not judge from the vase paintings and reliefs, but in some of its forms it no doubt resembles the heavy roll found on so many terracottas.[420] In spite of the frequency with which this roll appears on the heads of children, it is impossible to determine in what way, and of what material it was made. The stephane, and the heavy roll too, are worn quite generally by children over six years of age, let us say, while they are found only rarely on the heads of very young ones.[421]

XXV A
XXXI B

X E
XIII B

XVIII C
XXXV C

A considerable number of terracotta figures of boys show this same roll, apparently used as the foundation for a sort of small hat.[422] In shape this closely resembles a tam, since it is fairly flat on top, and its outer edge extends just a trifle beyond the roll. Exactly how it was fitted or fastened to the head, however, it is not easy to discover.

XXXVIII B

Girls, too, wear hats upon occasion, when dressed for a promenade, possibly.[423] These have a flat stiff brim, with rather a high peak on top. The effect, in combination with the long chiton, and the gracefully draped himation, is undeniably pretty. The kerchief[424] appears now and then on a girl's head, just as it is worn by women. Ordinarily the widest part is at the back of the head, and the ends are fastened in front over the forehead.

XXXVIII A
XXXVIII C

Ornaments are worn by girls in the ears, and around the neck and
arms. Eardrops are represented rather simply, in the shape of a
small ball,[425] or of a ring,[426] and where a necklace occurs it is of the
plainest sort.[427] Bracelets show greater variety, for we find either a
single ring,[428] or a serpent coiled several times about the arm.[429]
Now and then a girl carries a leaf-shaped fan to complete her costume;[430] in one case it may be the mother's fan with which the
youngster is playing.[431]

One garment which is curiously modern in appearance is a coat,
worn as the sole garment by small boys in a number of illustrations.[432]
The sleeves are, with two exceptions,[433] long, and it is generally open
in front. One drawing, only, shows the edges held by a cord, carefully laced back and forth.[434]

A description of children's footwear is a comparatively simple
matter, for often there are no signs of any at all. Part of this is
undoubtedly due to careless execution, but many of the children,
especially the smaller ones, are clearly intended to be barefoot.
Both sandals and shoes were in favor, however, and the former can be
observed to best advantage on boys' feet, where the garments did not
hang so low as to conceal the lacing. Since this was indicated often
by means of paint, especially on terracottas, only those examples
which are best preserved give us any adequate idea of it.[435] Where the
lines cross not only the foot, but above the ankle as well, we seem to
have not a mere sandal, but a sort of shoe, cut out so as to leave the
front of the ankle and the top of the foot bare. One grave relief, however, shows clearly a girl's sandals, with a suggestion of some rosette
ornament on the thong which passed between the first and second
toes.[436] Where girls' shoes are visible[437] one sees simply a rather thick
sole and the outline of the uppers, without any real indication as to
either their shape or height.

XXXVIII C

XIII B
XXXVI C
XXXVIII C

Front. C
XXXIX D

XXXIX A

XXXIX C

IX C

SICKNESS AND DEATH

Of children's physical ills we gain no knowledge from the objects which have been observed; an artist naturally would not choose such subjects for representation. One exception to this statement should, however, be mentioned, namely the monument of the physician Iason.[438] In this relief we see the man himself, massaging the swollen stomach of a boy who stands in front of him and turns his head to look up into the doctor's face.

Just as here, so too in a large number of other monuments, the child is an incidental, though rather important, figure. I have in mind those numerous reliefs where one parent, the deceased, is seated. Among the figures grouped around, there is often a small child, scarcely able to stand perhaps, but trying very hard to touch the mother's hand which is resting on her lap.[439] Children somewhat larger usually lean against the mother's knees,[440] or hold up some object for her to see.[441]

XXXVII B

XXXVII A

There are a limited number of grave stelai, for the older children, on which we see them represented exactly as the adults generally are, either with a servant beside them,[442] or clasping hands in farewell as they face each other.[443] One monument of this type is unusual because of its inscription, rather than for the relief itself.[444] A girl, quite large, stands holding a bird, by its wings, in her lowered left hand. On the ground is a small boy, reaching for the bird with both hands, exactly as we see the children doing on so many grave stelai for adults. The inscription runs as follows:

IX C

"Fate hath these parents cruelly bereft;
Yet they've through art some consolation left.
The sculptor's art retrieves each loved one's face,

Showing them, as in life, its wonted grace.
E'en the dark house of Hades cannot seize
For aye Mnesagora and Nikochares."

The most general type of monument for a child has already been referred to in several places. It is a relief of the child only, with its pet dog or bird, and with a plaything such as a ball, a rattle, a doll, or a toy cart. In other words, we still see these children just as their parents wished to visualize and recall them to mind. In some children's graves at Athens there were actually found the bones of birds, in one case enclosed in a small black pyxis.[445] This indicates that the child's pet, as well as some of its toys, might be buried with it. The same thing is clear from a white lekythos[446] showing a small boy sitting on the rocky shore, waiting for Charon's boat. A woman standing near him holds a large bird, such as a heron, and on the ground we see a box, apparently containing his playthings, which are to accompany him on his journey. He is not looking at his mother, however, but his face is turned, and his right hand is extended, toward Charon.

The delicately painted scenes on these white lekythoi show much the same restrained grief which is always observed in the grave reliefs, yet they often touch one deeply. There is, at the same time, a greater variety of presentation.

Though the Greek artist rarely represented a corpse, we see that of a very small child on one lekythos[447] carried to the grave by a female figure. On the other side of the picture stands a young man, resting a distaff on the base of the stele; it seems that he is the husband, and that his wife, the mother of the small child, has only recently died. Another such lekythos[448] shows the figure of a larger child carried on the arms of a woman. There have been found, also, a number of small sarcophagi for children. They vary in length, but one of the smallest measures only fifty six centimeters, or twenty two inches.[449]

Another of the vases[450] shows the unusual scene of a boy pursued by a large serpent. As he runs he looks back, with left hand extended as though to ward it off, while in his uplifted right he holds what looks like a stone. Has the painter told us here that the boy died as the result of the snake's bite?

On one lekythos[451] we see only the boy standing on the shore, with Charon already holding out one hand to help him into the boat. Another painting[452] shows not only the boy waiting, but behind him there stands a woman; on one hand she holds a box or tray, and in the other a fillet—offerings, doubtless, to be made at the boy's grave.

One more scene[453] will complete the list. Here the boy, again on *XL B* the shore, is a very small one, holding the pole of his toy cart with the left hand. Charon is approaching in his boat, but in this case it is not at him that the boy is looking. His face is turned back, and his free hand is extended toward his mother who stands near, powerless to hold him back from his journey.

"Hades, god unyielding, who heeds not the prayers of man,
Why, for our babe Kallaischros, did'st end life's little span?
Soon, in Persephone's dwelling, the goddess' plaything he;
Grievous sorrow unending our lot at home will be."[454]

NOTES

ABBREVIATIONS IN THE NOTES

In the case of a few museums, which offer only a limited amount of material on this subject, references are given in full in the notes. For all others, the following abbreviations will be used:

Athens, National Museum	A
——— Ceramicus	Cer
Berlin, Staatliche Museen	B
——— University, Archäologisches Seminar	BU
Boston, Museum of Fine Arts	Bo
Broomhall, Elgin Collection	BE
Brussels, Musées royaux du Cinquantenaire	Br
Cambridge, Mass. Fogg Museum	Ca
Chaeronea	Ch
Chicago, Art Institute	Chi
Copenhagen, National Museum	C
——— Glyptothek	CG
Dresden, Albertinum	D
Frankfurt-am-Main	F
Hamburg, Museum f. Kunst und Gewerbe	H
Istanbul, Musées des Antiquités	I
Leningrad, Hermitage	LH
London, British Museum	L
Madrid, Museo Arqueológico Naçional	Ma
Munich, Museum f. Antike Kleinkunst	M
——— Glyptothek	MG
Naples, Museo Nazionale	N
New York, Metropolitan Museum	NY
Oxford, Ashmolean Museum	O
Paris, Louvre	P
Philadelphia, University of Pennsylvania	PU
Providence, R. I. School of Design	Pr
Rome, Museo Nazionale	R
——— Vatican Museum	RV
Syracuse, Museo Archeologico	S
Toronto, Royal Ontario Museum	T
Tübingen	Tb
Vienna, Kunsthistorisches Museum	V
——— Museum f. Kunst und Industrie	VM
Würzburg, Martin von Wagner Museum	W
Yale University, New Haven	Y
vase	v
terracotta	t
marble	m
bronze	b

NOTES

1. Volo 1 painted marble.
2. A 5891 t, 12649 t.
3. A 991 m, 3376 m, 1158 v; Cleveland 25.1342 m.
4. M 5960 t.
5. D ZV3021 t; S Room XV t.
6. A 12981 t; N 110341 t; Rome Villa Borghese LXXI m.
7. A 12591 v; B TC.4996 t; Cer Nikandra stele; L 2232 m.
8. Palermo Mus. Naz. t.
9. NY 06.1021.144 v.
10. Volo Rhodion stele (Cf. also note 1).
11. B TC.7196 t; P AO-6540 t; Thebes Philotira stele.
12. D ZV1437 t; I 2711 t, 2712 t.
13. I 2384 t; N CS384 t; NY 10.210.81 terracotta mould.
14. L C278 t; N CS26 t; P C5090 t.
15. A 4838 t; B TC.7023 t; Bo 01.7747 t.
16. F 232 t; NY 17.190.2061 t; Pr 25.088 v.
17. Chalcis 790 t; D H⁴24i t; P CA2161 t.
18. A 3978 t; B TC.7428 t.
19. A 1021 m (I. G. II⁵ 4284 b).
20. A 978 m (I. G. II³ 4050).
21. A 993 m (I. G. II³ 2343).
22. R 14923 t.
23. BU e11 t; L B106 t; N 20923 t.
24. Olympia 74 t.
25. RV (Mus. Gregor. II, 83, 1a).
26. A 5620 t; Bo 01.7826 t; Orchomenos, Boeotia (Monastery Church) m.
27. A 5467 t; B TC.5199 t; I 1307 t.
28. M 5182 t, 6672 t.
29. P 335 t.
30. P D260 t.
31. B TC.8457 t.
32. A 5890 t, 5891 t; W t.
33. B 2209 v; Br 890 v; L E590 v.
34. P 403 t.
35. B TC.8347 t.
36. Anth. P. VI, 309.
37. L E590 v; M 2462 v; A 4419 t (slave).
38. L 878 b, 879 b.
39. Dar.-Sgl. fig. 2064. For the description and the photograph of the Olynthian rattle, which is as yet unpublished, I am indebted to Professor David M. Robinson of Johns Hopkins University.

40. Eleusis 314 t.
41. Heidelberg, Archäologisches Institut der Universität K14 v.
42. Pollux IX, 127.
43. A 11957 t; L C322 t; NY CP856 t.
44. BU E2 t; D ZV2814 t; L A446 t; M 425 t.
45. H 266 t.
46. LH t (Compte-rendu de la Commission impériale archéologique, 1874 p. 7).
47. B Inv.30659 t.
48. A 1268 v, 748 m, 2003 m; NY 11.100 m.
49. A 1158 m.
50. L 588.
51. Y 1913.453 t.
52. Berlin "Museum in der Prinz-Albrecht-Strasse" 497 t; L C887 t; NY CP488 t.
53. BU D356 t.
54. B TC.2717 t; Ma 11855 t; M 3126-3130 t; Nauplia 175 t.
55. L Life Coll., Case J.
56. B 2443 v; Bo 95.50 v; L E219 v; V 424 v.
57. M 5606 t; P AO-6540 t.
58. A 1023 m; H Inv.995 t; L C278 t; Thebes Philotira stele.
59. A lebes gamikos; Thebes 42 m.
60. A 12771 v; Bo 81.299 t; O Case 2.15 t.
61. S Room XVI t.
62. L E549 v; Ma 11566 v; New York Gallatin Coll. v; Tb 1400 v; W 2849 v.
63. L E396 v.
64. Bo 95.49 v.
65. A 5035 t; Candia 142 ivory; Ch 445 t; Nauplia 368 t.
66. O Case 2.13 t.
67. Bo 02.38 t; Chalcis 748 t.
68. A 1861 m.
69. Ca t; (Cf. NY 13.225.2 b).
70. Bo 10.170 b.
71. Bo 03.863 v; I 2494 v; L E282 v; Y 1913.142 v; M 2461 v.
72. B 2950 v; (Cf. Monum. Ined. IX pl. VII, 1).
73. John Chrysostom, Homily XII on 1 Corinthians. Ed. Ben. Tom. X p. 107 A-B.
74. B 2395 v.
75. L F223 v.
76. NY CS970 stone.
77. A 2220 v; B 2422 v, 4982 v; M 849 v; NY 21.88.80 v; P MNB1157 v.
78. Br Mousonis stele; NY CS986 stone, 26.60.89 m.
79. A 4459 t, 5896 t; Corinth t; P 197 t; Volo Case 3 t.
80. NY CP883 t.
81. A 14481 t.
82. NY CP2903 t.
83. NY CP2904 t, CP2907 t.

84. NY CP2903 t, CP2905 t, CP2906 t, CP2913 t.
85. D ZV1064 limestone.
86. L B73 t.
87. T 535 stone; V 62 t; Rome Barracco Museum 68 stone (Goddess?).
88. I 2937 t, 2938 t; L B30 t; N 20358 t; NY CP2899 t.
89. P S789 t.
90. NY CP2897 t.
91. N 20960 t.
92. A 4944 t; Br t; P C5103 t.
93. L B350 t.
94. L B68 t.
95. L B67 t.
96. A 4457 t, 4458 t; B TC.6344 t; I 2940 t; L B69 t.
97. L A184 t, A223 t; P S816 t; T 540 t, 541 t.
98. Bo 01.7773 t; L A182 t; P S811 t; T C543 t.
99. A 4876 t; Ch 468 α'-θ' t; I 3324 t; L 1797 t; P C4663 t, C4699 t.
100. Br R495 t; I 2941 t; L B70 t.
101. A 4874 t; Br A67 t; Ch 468ι'-$\iota\beta'$ t; L B95-97 t.
102. I 1828 t; N 85366 t; T C554 t; V 2130 t.
103. A 10413 t; L B(?) t.
104. I 3478 t; N 85355 t; P E456 t; T C557 t.
105. L Life Coll. t, B72 t.
106. L B303-305 t.

107. Br A2678 t.
108. L 1860 b, 1869 b.
109. A 5257 t; Ch 464α'-$\iota\epsilon'$ t, 467 α'-$\iota\beta'$ t; I 2946-8 t; L A238 t; N 85358 t; P N4434 t.
110. A 722 m; Chalcis 31 m; Tegea 1358 m.
111. A 695 m; Ch Anasiphron stele; NY 27.45 m.
112. A 2119 m; NY 12.159 m; Piraeus 17 m.
113. A 981 m; I 869 m; Leyden 254 m.
114. Aulus Gellius, Noctes Atticae X, 12.
115. Pollux IX, 107.
116. A 5901 t, 12468 v; Thebes 1651 m.
117. M 5446 t; O Case 2.17 t; P 387 t.
118. A 5739 t; L C747 t; M 6784 t.
119. Bo 01.7720 t; O Case 2.17 t; P 308 t.
120. A 4860 t, 4989 t; N 113362 t; S Room XV t.
121. A 5365 t; I 2709 t; M 5447 t; NY 06.1087 t.
122. CG 173b m.
123. A 1654 v.
124. BE v.
125. L 664 v.
126. A 771 m; CG 194 m.
127. I 257 m; NY 15.166 v.
128. Br A1904 v.
129. Bo 01.8086 v; P MNB1157 v.

130. Chi 07.14 v.
131. Bo 95.54 v.
132. B 2423 v.
133. A 1023 m, 2775 m, 4819 t, 1814 v. (Cf. also Conze 816).
134. A 4929 t; Bo 01.7721 t; I 2687 t; M 6778 t.
135. I 2493 v; M 6779 t; N 20934 t, 113361 t.
136. A 4681 t; D ZV1437 t; P C4722 t; V 89 t.
137. Ca 2289 plastic vase.
138. A 4827 t; N 20302 t.
139. L C751 t.
140. A 4736 t.
141. A 4930 t.
142. Br A906 v; L E527 v; NY 06.1021.196 v.
143. B TC.5195 t; Ca 24.08 v; P MNC841 m.
144. A 5361 t; I 2695 t; S Room XXI t.
145. L 649 m, E172 v. (Cf. also Conze 362).
146. A 12141 v; Bo 01.7727 t; N 113364 t.
147. A 2543 v; B TC.4986 t; O Case 2.15 t; P C4713 t.
148. I 2939 t; L E172 v; P S792 t; Piraeus t.
149. P C5028 t; R t.
150. Br A316 t; N 20935 t; NY 19.192.75 t.
151. P CA84 t.
152. R t.
153. I 2714 t; L D368 t; M 6782 t; P 314 t.
154. N 20361 t.
155. A 1320 v; C Case 71 v; D ZV1053 t.
156. A 4364 t; NY 21.88.80 v; P CA16 v.
157. L E485 v.
158. Bo 01.8071 v.
159. P 580 v.
160. L E589 v; M 2423 v.
161. A 4893 t, 14869 t.
162. A 4965 t; Bo 10.182 v; P 312 t.
163. A 13031 v; B 2419 v; O Case 2R v; Pr 25.067 v.
164. A 14534 v; Tb 1383 v; V 634 v.
165. CG 229a m; D ZV2600 m; Volo 652 m.
166. P MNB577 t.
167. A 5255 t; P 112 t.
168. W 1465 v.
169. Kiel v (Collection of Professor Eduard Schmidt).
170. L F101 v.
171. Venice Mus. Arch. 5 m.
172. I Room 26 Case 12 t.
173. P (Conze 1986) m.
174. D ZV800 t.
175. Chi 07.13 v; L E534 v; M 2459 v; Thebes toy vase.
176. Vienna v (Ber. d. Sächs. G. d. Wissenschaft, 1854, p. 247, pl. XIII).
177. Leyden 1905 Cat. XVIII, 25 v.

178. A 12822 v; B 2421 v, 2659 v, 4982 v; M 2459 v.
179. L E536 v. (Cf. Chi 07.13 v).
180. Tb 1380 v.
181. A 1321 v; B 3291 v.
182. Br A2319 v; L Life Coll. v.
183. New York Gallatin Coll. v.
184. A 1561 v, 1562 v; Bologna Mus. Civ. v; M 2461 v; NY 06.1021.202 v.
185. A 12141 v; Ma 19516 t; NY 21.88.80 v.
186. Anth. P. VI, 312.
187. Edinburgh Nat. Gallery (Conze 817) m; A 776 m.
188. A 2103 m, 2771 m, 2775 m; Avignon 31 m; MG 199 m.
189. A (Sybel 2045 = Conze 816) m, 1993 (Conze 882) m. In spite of Conze's suggestion (882) that the hand seen above the doll's head is held there merely to steady it, I believe that the position of the fingers supports my own view. In 816 there is, in fact, no hand visible under the doll's feet.
190. Epidaurus 38 stone.
191. Bo 98.891 t; P CA573 t, CA623 t, CA1931 t; T C534 t.
192. A 5693 t; Bo 19.313 t; L C10 t; V 197 t.
193. L C3 t; N 20331 t, CS244 t; NY 11.212.43 bone.
194. Symposium 4, 55.

195. A 5836 t; Bo 18.460 t; Pr 22.108 t; VM 891 t.
196. L C462 t; NY 20.205 t, 26.60.49 t. (Cf. reliefs: A 2771 m; MG 199 m).
197. B TC.6833 t; I 1903-7 t; L C522 t; NY 18.96 t; V 196 t.
198. L 599 t.
199. Br. Mus. A Guide to Greek and Roman Life. 1920. p. 196.
200. A 1456 v; B 2406 v; NY 15.25 v.
201. NY 23.73.1.
202. NY 06.1021.142a-b, 06.1021.154a-b.
203. A 1672, 10454; Chalcis 848; L E552.
204. NY GR1212.
205. A 12410 t.
206. A 12410 t; Chalcis 845 t.
207. A 12410 t.
208. A 12992 t.
209. A 12613 t.
210. A 12614 t.
211. A 12615 t.
212. L B313 t; NY 10.210.77 t.
213. A 4877 t, 12612 t; Bo 01.7766 t; I 3044 t; NY 12.232.20 t; P Myrina 334 t.
214. A 12409 t; Ch 475a'-ε' t; Delphi 4320 t.
215. NY CP2901.
216. A 1245 t, 5977 t, 12408 t.
217. M 5324 t; P CA597 t.
218. M 6671 t.

219. NY CP2848.
220. P 665 t.
221. A 11120 t.
222. A 4664 t, 4665 t; Bo 01.7869 t; M 5386 t.
223. S Room XII Case VIII v.
224. L B314 t.
225. G. van Hoorn, De Vita atque Cultu Puerorum, p. 78.
226. A 10449 t; L A519 t.
227. A 420 t, 421 t; Bo 99.536 t; P CA446 t, CA447 t.
228. Athen. Mitth. XV (1890) p. 374.
229. Baltimore Johns Hopkins Univ. Mus. v; Br 891 v; NY GR588 v; W v.
230. N 113355 t.
231. B Inv.3168 v.
232. M 2674 v.
233. A 884 m; Geneva No. I 651 v; L E296 v; O 300 v.
234. A 14705 v; L Life Coll. v; NY 23.160.55 v.
235. Bo 01.7860 t.
236. M 2674 v.
237. L 663 v.
238. L 621 Life Coll. (Cf. astragals on Amynten stele: Arch. Jahrb. XX (1905) p. 78, no. 17, pl. 5).
239. L 621 Life Coll.
240. Bo 01.7798-9 t, 03.897 t; NY 06.1021.119 v.
241. Pollux IX, 126

242. L D161 t.
243. Bo 01.7798-9 t.
244. Bo 01.7841 t; L E537 v; M 6760 t.
245. Anth. P. VI, 308.
246. P CA1734 t.
247. Pollux IX, 102.
248. Pollux IX, 101; Plato, Lysis 206E.
249. L 622 Life Coll.
250. A 723 m, 1040 m; Athens Private House (Conze 462) m.
251. Chi 07.16 v; L E548 v, E549 v.
252. I 2330 t; NY 07.286.18 t, 11.212.29 t; W H612 v.
253. B 2488 v; W H588 v.
254. Bo 03.818 v; L E606 v.
255. L E606 v; W H588 v. (Cf. B TC.8327 t).
256. Tb 1632a-b v.
257. NY 06.1021.119 v.
258. BE v; NY 25.78.48 v.
259. M 1827 v.
260. L E467 v.
261. L B182 v; O 250 v.
262. Athens Private Coll(?) v. (Benndorf, Griechische Vasenbilder, pl. 37, 5).
263. C. Robert, Gr. Kinderspiele auf Vasen. Arch. Zeitung 1879, p. 81.
264. B 2417 v.
265. Pollux IX, 119.

266. B TC.3570 t; CG T11 t; NY 07.286.4 t; P C5043 t; VM 802 t.

267. A 3476 m.

268. A 3477 m.

269. Élite Mon. Cer. IV, pl. 79 v (Hamilton Coll.?); L 1039 silver ring; Vienna 305 gem.

270. Monumenti, Annali e Bulletini 1855, pl. VI v.

271. Plutarch, Agesilaus XXV, 5.

272. Skimatari 20 m.

273. Clarac, Musée pl. 712, no. 1696.

274. Bo 10.191a-b v; Ma 11128 v.

275. L E387 v.

276. NY 13.232.3 v.

277. B 2394 v, 2589 v; M 234 v.

278. N 81497 v.

279. L F223 v; N 2066 v; RV small oinochoe. For a description of a similar modern toy see The American Boy's Book of Sports and Games. New York, Dick and Fitzgerald, 1864, p. 463 The Water-cutter.

280. B 2549 v. For a modern parallel cf. note 279, p. 464 The Bandilor.

281. A 2192 t, 2350 t; NY 28.167 t.

282. For this interesting suggestion I am indebted to Prof. C. H. Young. Cf. note 279, p. 53 The Sucker.

283. B 945 m; Paris Dzialynski Coll.(?) v. (Cf. Bo 96.716 b; M 805 v).

284. N 2574 v; Paris Dzialynski Coll.(?) v.

285. NY 06.1021.197 v.

286. NY 07.260 bronze mirror.

287. Bo 01.8024 v.

288. W v.

289. NY 10.210.18 v.

290. L E629 v.

291. A 4927 t; Bo 81.306 v, 95.53 v.

292. I m (G. Mendel, Catalogue des Sculptures, v. II, no. 554).

293. A 1322 v; NY 09.221.40 v.

294. O Case 2R v.

295. A 14527 v.

296. T C370 v.

297. Herodotus VI, 129. Suggested by Dr. Robert Zahn.

298. A 4818 t. (Cf. A 1915 m, 1980 m).

299. B TC.6289 t, TC.8033 t.

300. Ma 10924 v.

301. L E653 v.

302. L E90 v.

303. NY (G. M. A. Richter, Catalogue of Engraved Gems, no. 28).

304. Bo 10.227 t.

305. NY 08.258.24 v.

306. Athen. Mitth. II, pl. 16; Clarac Musée II, p. 703 pl. 212, 257; MG 206 m.

307. PU 2448 v.
308. J. H. S. XXIX, p. 362.
309. L A431 t; Pr 06.051 t.
310. Athenaeus X, 10 p. 437C-D.
311. Philostratus, Heroica XII, 2 p. 314.
312. A 14509 v; B 2420 v; Bo 02.40 v; NY 06.1021.198 v.
313. A 1234 v, 2146 v; M 2460 v; P MNB3061 v.
314. A 1266 v, 1560 v; Bo 02.40 v; L E551 v.
315. A 1226 v; B 2658 v; L E536 v; T 370 v.
316. A 1228 v, 1268 v, 1353 v, 2544 v; L E550 v.
317. A 1557 v, 1612 v, 14533 v; B 2659 v; NY 06.1021.202 v.
318. A 1561 v, 11737 v, 12822 v; B 2659 v; L E550 v.
319. A 1266 v, 1561 v, 11737 v. (Cf. Bologna Mus. Civ. oinochoe).
320. L E551 v.
321. A 1321 v.
322. NY 24.97.34 v.
323. B 2658 v.
324. NY 06.1021.196 v.
325. A 1222 v.
326. L 553 v. (Cf. Br A2318 v for torch).
327. Br A906 v; M 2470 v.
328. A 4852 t.
329. M 5441 t.
330. L 604 Life Coll.
331. L 605 Life Coll.
332. L 607 Life Coll. (Iliad I, 468 ff.).
333. NY 14.2.4 (four leaves) from Egypt.
334. Herondas III, 14-16.
335. L 609 Life Coll.
336. NY CB236.
337. P MND757.
338. L Life Coll.
339. L Life Coll.
340. A 5026 t, 12634 t; B TC.7084 t; I 2744 t; Ma 19515 t.
341. Dittenb. Sylloge³ no. 578, 11.7-10.
342. NY 06.1021.167 v.
343. Br A980 t.
344. A 4889 t; L 602 Life Coll. t.
345. A 4862 t.
346. A 4683 t; B TC.8437 t; L C214 t; NY 23.259 t.
347. P 287 t.
348. A 4478 t, 14867 t; I 2533 t; NY 17.230.10 v.
349. Girls: A 5010 t; I 2627 t; L Life Coll. t, 533 chalcedony gem; P N4526 t, CA2160 t. Boys: BU E57 t; Br A1013 v; PU 4842 v.
350. W terracotta.
351. NY 20.226 t.
352. L 649 m.
353. NY 17.230.10 v.
354. B 2285 v; L E525 v.
355. B 2285 v.

356. A 14555 v.
357. Leyden 1875 v. (Cf. M 1101 v).
358. MG 481 m.
359. O vase fragment fr. Naukratis (J. H. S. 1905, pl. 6, 5).
360. B 2285 v.
361. B 2285 v. (Cf. L E172 v).
362. Bo 01.7788 t.
363. Bo 97.605 v, 95.51 v.
364. A 4851 t; B TC.8034 t; BU E10 t.
365. A (no number) t.
366. A 4171 t; Bo 10.230 t.
367. A 4841 t.
368. P 664 t.
369. A 1230 v.
370. A 4990 t.
371. L E527 v.
372. L E533 v.
373. A 1223 v.
374. L C527 t.
375. P 246 t.
376. A 12144 v.
377. B 2400 v.
378. L E185 v; S Room XIII v.
279. L E185 v.
380. NY 12.232.11 t.
381. A 4907 t.
382. Tb 1609 v.
383. W 139 v.
384. LH 875 v.
385. B 6918 gem (Furtw. Antike Gemmen, pl. 42, 50).

386. Herondas III, 59-61.
387. A 2367 m; Bo 87.394 t; Chalcis 790 t; F 232 t.
388. A 97 m; C Case 71 v; Ma 11566 v; Piraeus toy vase.
389. A 1561 v, 12822 v; Bologna Mus. Civ. v(Élite Mon. Cer. II, pl. 89).
390. A 2083 m, 3289 m; NY 12. 159 m.
391. NY 19.192.5 t; V 90 t; N 20297 t(held by mother).
392. I 2685 t, 2384 t; M 849 v; P C4998 t.
393. A 2863 m, 1032 t; Ch 447 t; L B61 t, D357 t; O Case 2.18 t. This costume is sometimes associated with slaves, as seen on the little figures with lanterns: N 20773 t, 110341 t; R 278 m. There seems no good reason for supposing, however, that the Greeks did not use this heavy garment to give protection to their own children during cold weather.
394. A 3305 m.
395. A 4655 t; NY 06.1096 t; Volo 298 painted stele.
396. A 4635 t; P 312 t; Pr 06.051 t.
397. Athens Monastery ton Asomaton m; A 776 m, 894 m.
398. A 4792 t; Bo 86.398 t; M 6767 t.
399. A 894 m, 981 m, 1017 m.

400. A 696 m, 1128 m, 2102 m, 2775 m; Tegea 1358 m.

401. A (Sybel 3294) m, 695 m, 892 m, 2003 m, 1305 m. The last was used as an illustration because of the clearness of detail, although she is considerably older than any of the others.

402. A 892 m, 1305 m.

403. A 4054 t, 4128 t; NY GR1243 v; P MNB479 t.

404. A 4125 t; Bo 01.7805 t, 10.116 b; D H⁴240 t.

405. L C298 t.

406. A 914 m, 4652 t; P MNB1521 t; V 138 t.

407. A 4130 t; D ZV75i t; L C321 t; NY 07.286.28 t.

408. A 4487 t; B 2357 v; Bo 01.7853 t; P CA2165 t.

409. B TC.7080 t; NY 06.1064 t; P 291 t, 338 t.

410. A 6071 t, 913 m, 3289 m; B TC.5195 t; V 330 t.

411. A 4795 t, 175 m, 748 m; Chalcis 748 t; M 798 t.

412. Bo 10.230 t; I 2686 t, 2695 t; M 6779 t.

413. A 4792 t; Br Mousonis stele; D ZV93 t; P 112 t.

414. L D161 t; NY 06.1021.119 v, 11.141 m; Tb 1632a-b v.

415. A 777 m; Bo 01.7805 t; Delphi 3333 m; NY 19.192.7 t.

416. M 6575 t, 6762 t; Rome Palazzo Grazioli b (Brunn-Bruckmann, Denkmäler Gr. und Röm. Skulptur, no. 540).

417. A 722 m; Cer Eukoline stele.

418. A 1232 v, 12142 v, 4913 t; M 2467 v.

419. A 981 m, 1128 m, 1146 m; MG 199 m; Palermo Philokrates stele.

420. Bo 03.903 t; M 5445 t; Nauplia 500 t; P S1635 t.

421. The suggestion made by van Hoorn that this roll, or the stephane, was worn low on the forehead by smaller children, to protect them in case of a fall, finds very little support in the material observed.

422. A 4046 t; D ZV735 t; L t; NY 06.1064 t.

423. A 4054 t; M 6762 t; Nauplia 527 t.

424. A 831 m (sketch of lost part in Conze 289); L Xanthippos stele.

425. Bo 03.897 t; M 2466 v, 5422 t, 5408 t.

426. Cer Eukoline stele.

427. Cer Eukoline stele; M 2466 v.

428. M 2466 v; P MNC841 m.

429. A (Conze 1921) m; NY 26.60.89 m.

430. A 4174 t; L C298 t; M 6762 t.

431. A 1028 m.

432. A 1224 v, 5069 t; NY 06.1021.196 v. For older girls wearing coats, cf. Bologna Mus. Civ. v; BE stele (Conze 819).

433. Br A2318 v; Stackelberg Gräber der Hellenen, pl. XVII.

434. A 1226 v.

435. B TC.7080 t; L 334 t; NY GR1243 v; P MR1514 b.

436. Athens Monastery ton Asomaton m.

437. A 981 m, 2102 m, 2775 m.

438. L 629 m.

439. A 2081 m, 3289 m; Piraeus stele.

440. A 2083 m, 3465 m; Br A1310 m; Piraeus stele (Conze 60).

441. A 722 m, 762 m; Br A1315 m.

442. A 934 m; 1017 m, 1305 m; Avignon Musée Calvet 31 m.

443. A 877 m; L 689 m.

444. Cf. note 436. I.G.II^3 3961. Translated by Prof. E. D. Perry.

445. Athen. Mitth. 1893, p. 175 sep. 168.

446. A 1814 v.

447. O v (J. H. S. 1895, p. 328 and fig. 2).

448. B 2447 v.

449. Leyden (1905 catalogue, X, 5).

450. NY GR600 v.

451. A 1758 v.

452. NY GR619 v.

453. NY 09.221.44 v.

454. Anth. P. VII, 483. Translated by Professor C. H. Young.

PLATES

A

B

C

D

I

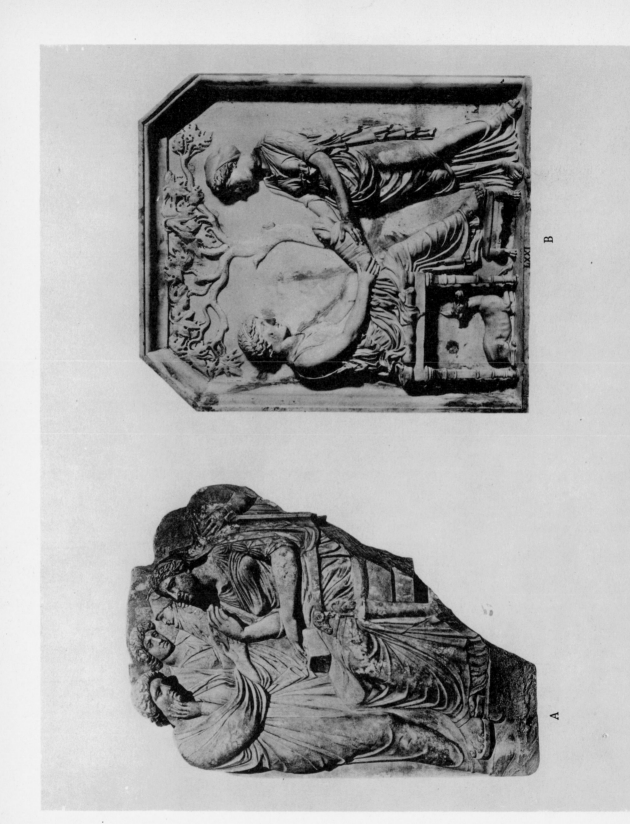

A

B

II

A

B

C

E

D

III

D

A

E

B

C

F

IV

A

B

C

D

V

A

B

VI

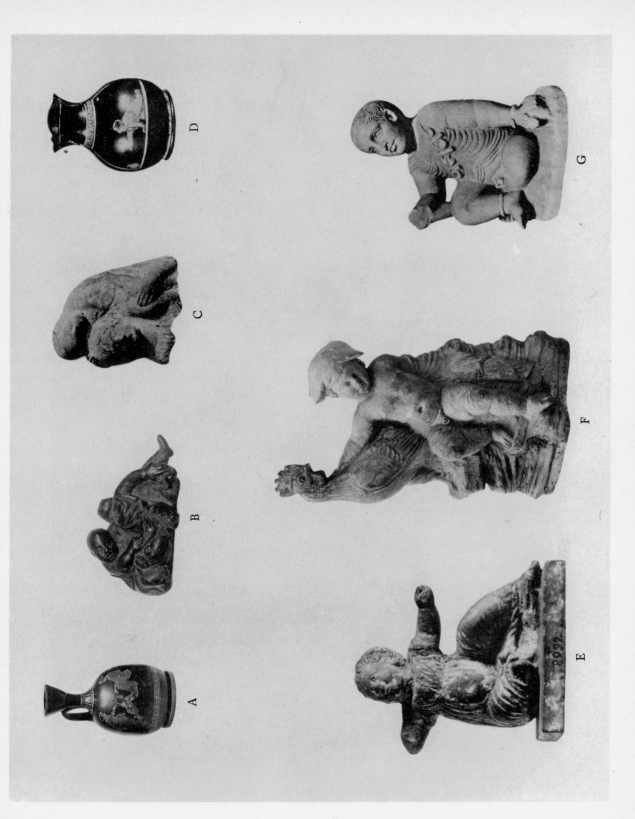

A   B   C   D

E   F   G

VII

VIII

A

C B

IX

A   B   C

D   E

X

A   B   C

E

D   F

XI

A   B   C

D   E

XII

A

B

C

D

E

F

XIII

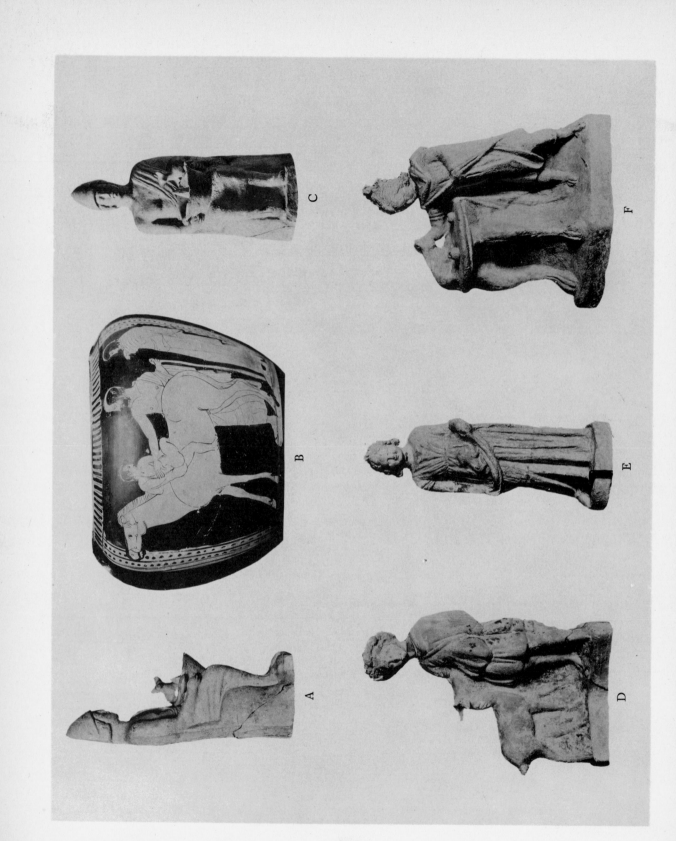

XIV

C

D

A

B

XV

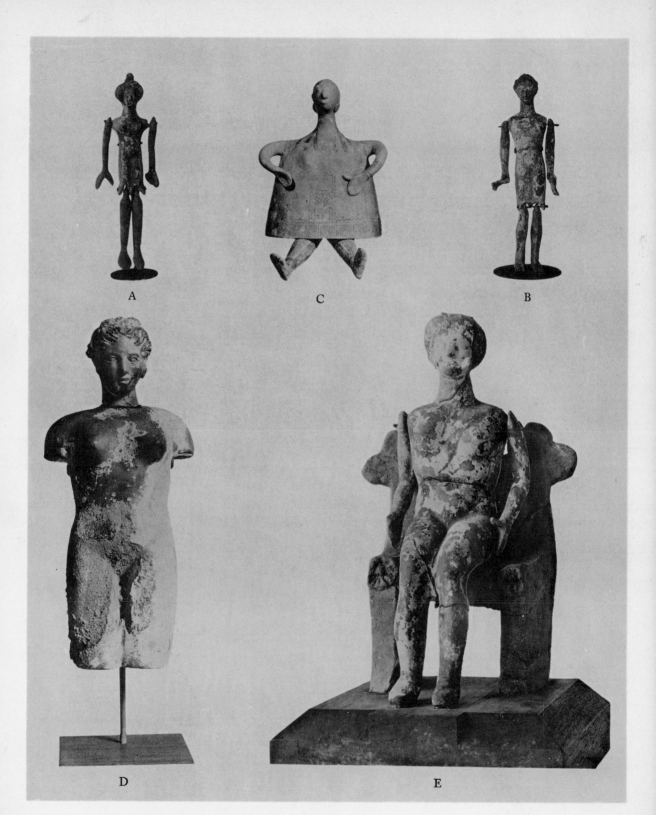

A   C   B

D   E

XVI

A

B

C

C

D

XVII

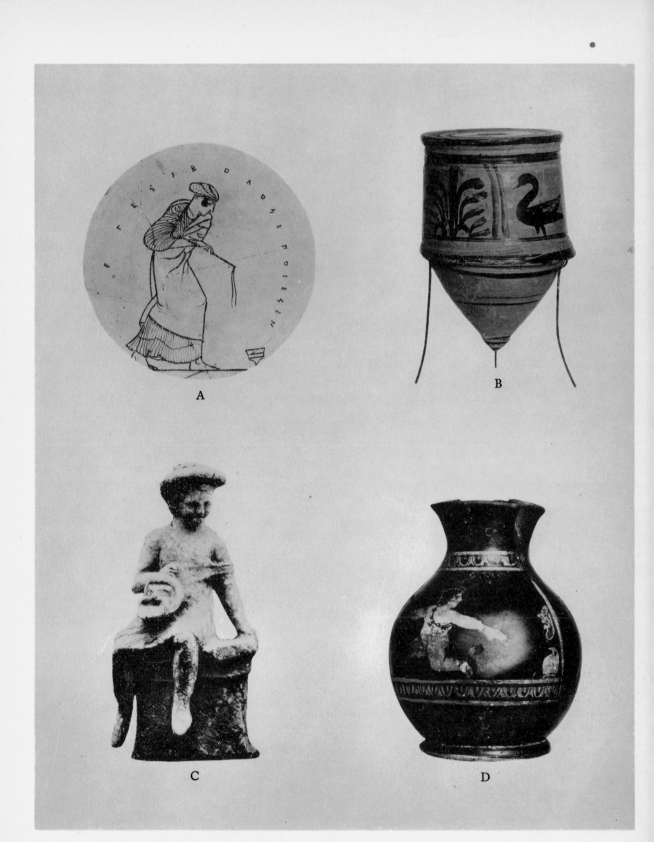

A   B

C   D

XVIII

A

B

C

D

XIX

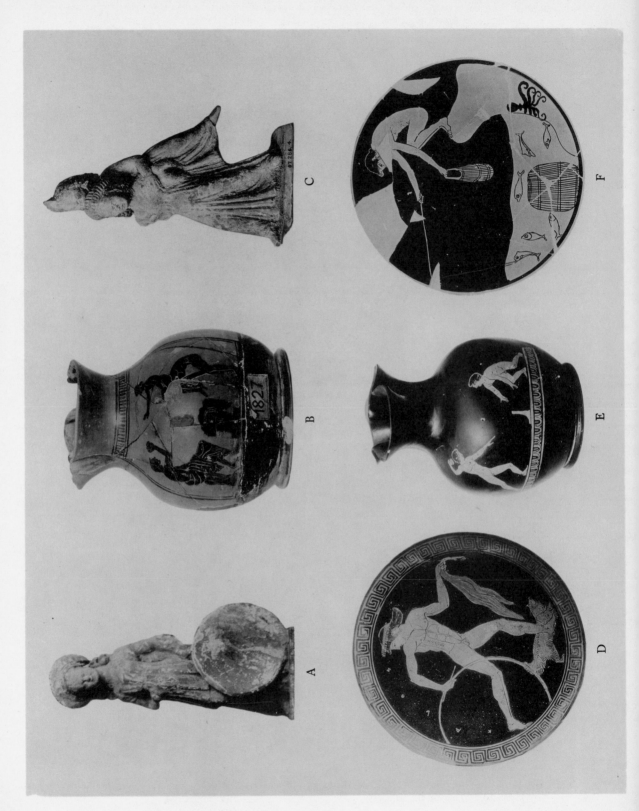

A

B

XXI

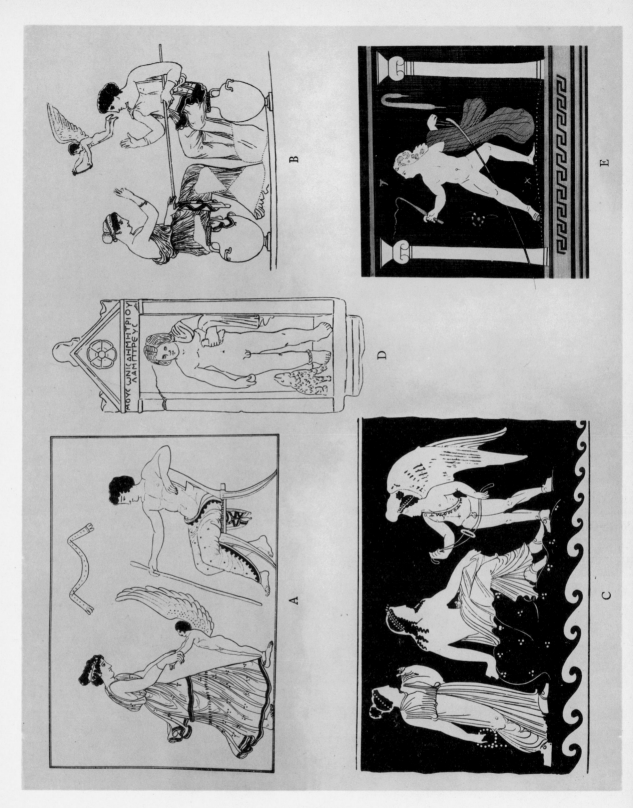

XXII

A

B

C

XXIII

A

B

C

E 653

D

XXIV

A   B   C

D   E

XXV

A

B

C

D

E

F

XXVI

XXVII

A   B   C

D   E

XXVIII

A

B

C

D

T.187.

XXIX

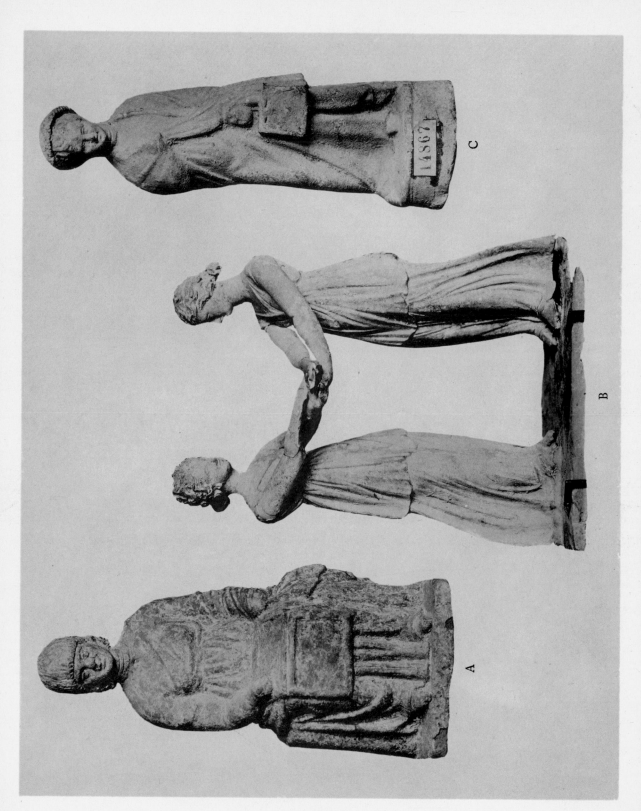

A   B   C

XXX

XXXI

A

B

C

D

XXXII

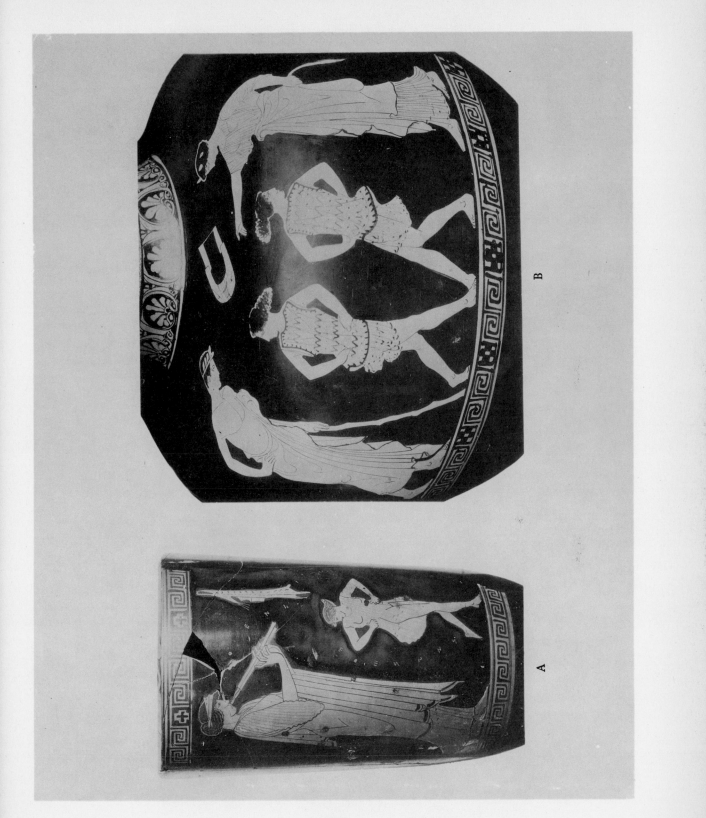

B

A

XXXIII

B

A

XXXIV

A

B

C

D

E

XXXV

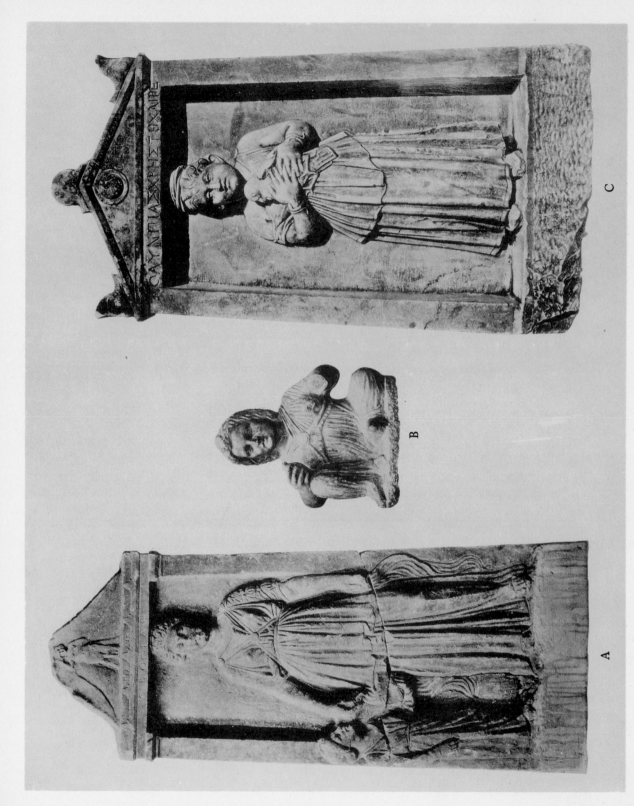

XXXVI

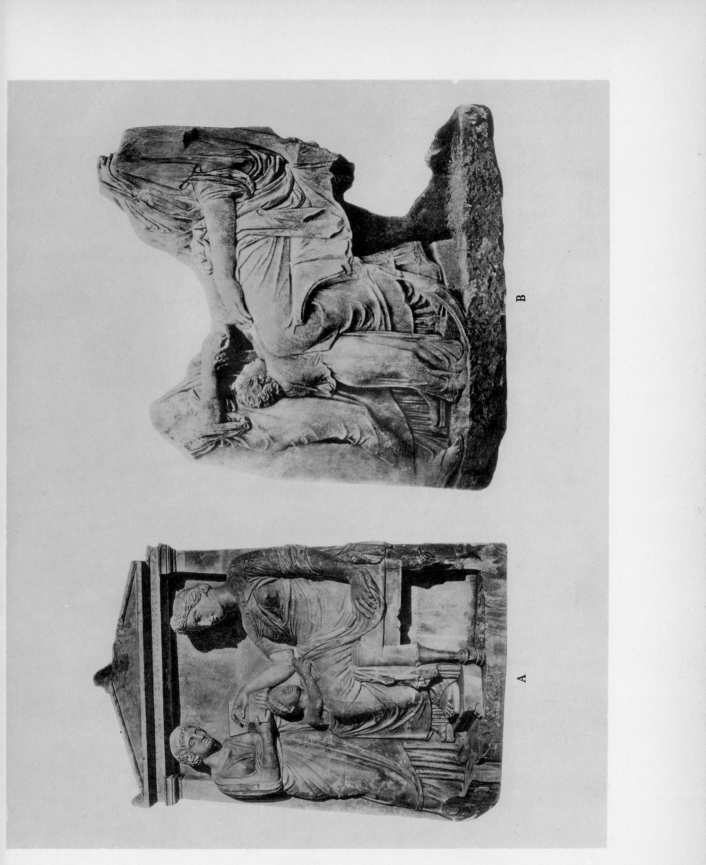

B

A

XXXVII

A

B

C

D

XXXVIII

A

B

C

D

XXXIX

A

B

XL

BIBLIOGRAPHY

Becq de Fouquieres, L. Les jeux des anciens. ed. II Paris 1873.

Conze, A. Die Attischen Grabreliefs. Berlin 1893-1922.

Deubner, L. Spiele u. Spielzeug der Griechen. Die Antike 1930.

Elderkin, Kate McK. Jointed dolls in antiquity. A.J.A. XXXIV no. 4 1930.

Grasberger, L. Erziehung u. Unterricht im kl. Altert. Würzburg 1864.

Heubach, D. Das Kind in der griech. Kunst. Diss. Heidelberg 1903.

Hoorn, G. van. De vita atque cultu puerorum monumentis antiquis explanato.
    Diss. Amsterdam 1909.

Καστριώτης, Π. Ἀνάγλυφα ἐπιτύμβια μετὰ πλαγγόνος. Ἐφ. Ἀρχ. 1909.

Ploss, H. Das kleine Kind vom Tragbett bis zum ersten Schritt. Berlin 1881.

Robert, C. Griechische Kinderspiele auf Vasen. Arch. Zeitung 1879.

Sanborn, A. L'enfant dans l'art antique. Le Musée I, 2.

INDEX

COLUMBIA UNIVERSITY PRESS
COLUMBIA UNIVERSITY
NEW YORK

———

FOREIGN AGENT
OXFORD UNIVERSITY PRESS
HUMPHREY MILFORD
AMEN HOUSE, LONDON, E.C.